BUSINESS
THROUGH THE EYES OF FAITH

OTHER BOOKS IN THIS SERIES:

BUSINESS THROUGH THE EYES OF FAITH

Richard C. Chewning
John W. Eby
Shirley J. Roels

Christian College Coalition

For Enduring Values

HarperSanFrancisco

A Division of HarperCollins*Publishers*

The Christian College Coalition is an association of Christian liberal arts colleges and universities across North America. More than 30 Christian denominations, committed to a variety of theological traditions and perspectives, are represented by our member colleges. The views expressed in this volume are primarily those of the author(s) and are not intended to serve as a position statement of the Coalition membership. For more information please contact the Christian College Coalition at 329 Eighth Street NE, Washington, DC 20002.

Unless otherwise noted, Scripture quotations in this publication are from the Holy Bible, New International Version. Copyright © 1973, 1978, 1984 International Bible Society. Used by permission of Zondervan Bible Publishers.

Scripture quotations marked NASB are from the New American Standard Bible. Copyright © The Lockman Foundation 1960, 1962, 1963, 1968, 1971, 1972, 1973, 1975.

Library of Congress Cataloging-in-Publication Data

Chewning, Richard C.
   Business through the eyes of faith / Richard C. Chewning, John W. Eby, Shirley J. Roels. — 1st ed.
     p.   cm.
   Includes bibliographical references.
   ISBN 0-06-061350-5
   1. Business—Religious aspects—Christianity.   I. Eby, John W. (John Wilmer)   II. Roels, Shirley J.   III. Title.
HF5388.C54   1990
261.8—dc20   89-45751
                                               CIP

94 95 96 97   RRD(H)   13 12 11 10 9 8 7 6 5

CONTENTS

FOREWORD

Suppose one looks at business through the eyes of Christian faith. What does one see? What questions come to mind? Which directions seem promising? Which practices call for disapproval? Can there be such a thing as a theology of business? It is to such questions as these that this book is addressed.

Almost from the beginnings of Christianity there have been Christians who have cast an eye of suspicion on business. The authors quote the comment of St. Jerome, "A merchant can seldom if ever please God." The question, then, what do faith and business have to do with each other, has long been on the agenda. To ask the question today, however, is to ask it concerning a very different kind of business from that which St. Jerome knew. Business in the modern world has become a relatively autonomous sector of society. It has a life of its own. The question is thus more complex, its answers less obvious, than it was in former ages.

The writers of this book—themselves successful practitioners and knowledgeable teachers of business—do not enter the discussion suspicious of business. On the contrary: they develop their understanding of business as an appropriate and even necessary part of our human calling on earth before the face of God. But neither are they apologists for business as is, or purveyors of simplistic slogans like "God is not against competition" or "God favors individual initiative." What characterizes the discussion can perhaps best be called "critical appreciation."

This critical appreciation is grounded in both an authentic spirituality and a thorough acquaintance with modern business. From this combination comes an unusually imaginative, humanly sensitive, and biblically responsive discussion of Christianity and business. Categories like justice, love, and shalom are put to work. Those who find themselves on the underside of business enter the picture as well as those who sit at the top. The impact of American business on the Third World is considered as well as its impact on America. The quality of the workplace is discussed along with the role of profits. Advertising is considered as well as production.

I have mentioned the combination of imagination and commitment in the discussion. What is also striking is what I can only call the "liberated" character of the discussion. To a remarkable degree, the authors have liberated themselves from ideologies of both the right and the left and looked with clear eyes of faith at this dimension of our existence, which so profoundly shapes the lives of all of us—modern business.

Naturally there are some questions, which the writers leave unanswered. There are others to which their answers may prove controversial. But whether you are a Christian or not, and whether you are engaged in business or only participate by way of consuming its products and employing its services—if, whatever your reason, you have wanted to know how modern business looks to some perceptive and informed Christians, you will, I think, find no better book than this giving you what you want.

Nicholas Wolterstorff
Professor of Philosophical Theology
Yale Divinity School

PREFACE

God calls us as Christians to look at all of life, including business, "through the eyes of faith." This means that we are called to see the world as God does. We look to biblical principles to guide our decisions and to form our values. When faced with tough questions, we ask, "What would Jesus do?" In difficult circumstances we examine Scripture and ask the Holy Spirit and other Christians for guidance. We want our lives to reflect wholeness and integrity.

We have written this book to help Christians integrate the tenets of faith with the practice of business. Consequently we do not focus on business institutions, but on people who work in business. God calls many of us to work in the business arena and has strong interest in our business-related attitudes, motives, and behavior. God's interests should be our interests.

Although this book was written primarily for college students studying business at Christian colleges, it does not fit neatly into the outline of a college curriculum or a business textbook. *Business Through the Eyes of Faith* does something far more important: it identifies a point of view and a set of biblical principles that Christians can apply to business activity. Knowing these biblical principles will help maturing Christians avoid the unintended error of using the Bible to justify what already has been decided, rather than properly allowing the Bible to shape what is to be decided. *Business Through the Eyes of Faith* does not merely apply biblical proof-texts to business problems; it illustrates the application of groups of scriptural texts, which form the heart of biblical principles.

This book will serve best when used in settings that facilitate discussion and interaction. A short vignette or case study is included at the beginning of each chapter to encourage discussion. Discussion questions are included at the end of each chapter. These questions are designed to raise important issues, to catch attention, and to stimulate thought. The vignettes and discussion questions do not imply specific answers, but serve as an open door and stimulus to further thinking. Sometimes the vignettes represent the point of view of the authors, and sometimes they do not. A teacher's guide with additional illustrations, discussion questions, and suggestions for further study is available from the Christian College Coalition at the address listed in the front of the book.

Many people have contributed in significant ways to the development of this book. Virginia Gero and Eileen Boonstra typed numerous drafts of the manuscript. Joyce Rutt Eby helped with the final editing. The Business Task Force members and the Series Advisory Board members provided valuable support, direction, and counsel. We particularly appreciate the patience, good advice, and continual reminders of the significance of this project provided by three Christian College Coalition staff members: John Dellenbach, John Bernbaum, and Karen Longman. Their encouragement and facilitation of vital meetings was crucial to the completion of this book. We express special appreciation to Christine Anderson from Harper & Row. Her insightful comments are deeply appreciated.

Business Through the Eyes of Faith has also benefited from the examination and suggestions of eighty faculty members of business departments at Christian colleges, who gathered during one week at Wheaton College for the primary purpose of offering their input to make this book as helpful as possible. The seriousness and tenacity of this group in reviewing the manuscript has contributed immensely to its clarity and strength.

Thanks!
Richard C. Chewning
John W. Eby
Shirley J. Roels

BUSINESS
THROUGH THE EYES OF FAITH

PART 1

The Big Picture: Business from a Christian Perspective

Chapter 1

BUSINESS: IS THERE A CHRISTIAN PERSPECTIVE?

POINT FOR DISCUSSION

Corporate Goals

Computer Management and Development Services (CMDS), in Harrisonburg, Virginia, develops, markets, and supports administrative management computer software for colleges, universities, and health care organizations. In 1987 it was listed by *Inc.* magazine as one of the fastest-growing privately held companies in North America. Its top management and many of its more than fifty employees are committed Christians. CMDS has adopted the following corporate goals.[1]

To Honor God

We believe that our Christianity is something that is a part of all we do. Therefore, we commit ourselves to operate CMDS within our understanding of Christian ethical and moral beliefs. We believe Christ should be honored by all that we do and say.

To Develop People

We believe that people employed by CMDS are our most important asset. We commit ourselves to pay fairly, treat one another honestly, and promote development of the individual. We believe that people we work for are also important and commit ourselves to training them in the operation of the system, treating them honestly, and assisting in the development of the individual in any way we can.

To Pursue Excellence in Service

Service is our most important product. We recognize the importance of service to our customers and commit ourselves to responding promptly to requests and/or problems. We will continue to refine and improve our products. Only by providing an important service to our customers will we continue to exist as a company. We commit ourselves to excellence.

To Make a Profit

We recognize the need to make a profit in order to operate a viable business. We are nonetheless committed to meet goals one, two, and three and will sacrifice a larger profit in order to meet these goals.

Business from a Biblical Perspective

A certain amount of tension between business and Christianity seems always to have existed. St. Jerome said, "A merchant can seldom if ever please God." St. Augustine, a fifth-century Christian bishop, wrote, "Business is in itself evil."

Most Christians today, however, would disagree. All around the world, in a wide variety of political and economic systems, Christians are involved in business. (Some see business merely as a way to make a living. Others, like those at CMDS, see it as an integral part of God's plan for meeting the needs of people.) If you agree with Augustine, you can stop reading now. If, instead, you think that business is one setting in which Christians can live out God's call, keep going. The statements by St. Augustine and St. Jerome are provocative, and they are quoted here to catch your attention. Many people think it is easy to be a Christian in business. It is not easy, but it is possible.

This book tackles some of the really important issues Christians face in business. It suggests that Christians approach business as part of God's work in the world. It argues that it is possible to be both ethical and successful, but that being ethical and Christian will not necessarily guarantee success.

A Christian approach to business is not a cookbook of simplistic recipes for resolving complex business problems. Certainly CMDS cannot expect the Bible to explicitly answer its questions about which new computer software products to develop, or which of several qualified employees to hire. The president of CMDS does not look to the Bible to find his business plan. Yet CMDS can employ a number of biblical principles, recurring scriptural themes, that provide sound and helpful guidelines for facing real business issues in the real world.

This in no way implies that biblical principles, such as "We are stewards and God is the ultimate titleholder," are easy to apply. Nor does it imply that every Christian will apply the principles the same way. For example, some Christians might use an unusually large profit from a successful year's operations to modernize capital equipment. Others might pay out an extra dividend to investors or share the profit with employees. God is concerned about workers, customers, and other stakeholders; but the responsibility for determining what is fair and what achieves business objectives in the light of biblical principles requires hard thinking, creative problem solving, and careful implementation.

The business environment is filled with uncertainty. Even though decision makers have the best intentions, the results are not always what they would want. This happened recently in a small community in eastern Pennsylvania. A firm there had been operated as a closely held corporation for two generations by committed Christians. They took very seriously their responsibility to run their business in a way that served the community, the employees, and customers who related to it. It had grown rapidly and had developed a good reputation among its employees and customers. The local newspaper did an article praising the founder for his humble Christian spirit. During the last several years the business faced economic difficulty that required it to seek a friendly merger with a larger firm with needed capital. This firm shared the values of the owners of the smaller firm, so the merger seemed like a good idea.

The larger firm, however, was traded on the open market. Soon after the merger, it was the target of a successful unfriendly takeover by a firm with very different values. The company changed dramatically. Many employees lost their jobs. Profit, not service, became the highest objective. The original owners were sadly disappointed. They had made the best decisions they knew how to make, but the results were not at all what they wanted. Uncertainties can sometimes alter the outcome of decisions so that there is little resemblance between the original intention and the actual result.

Making decisions in business is not a simple function of running anticipated actions through a formula or process. Decisions rest upon a vast array of judgments that require the integration of perceived facts and beliefs concerning technology, resources, markets, individuals, society, moral perceptions, and a host of other components. To function in a godly manner in the marketplace, we need all the wisdom that is available.

We are called to be like Christ and to think like he would think (Philippians 2:1–8). Christians know that this is made possible by the presence and inner work of the Holy Spirit, not by our efforts alone. We are called not only to know the will of God, but to do it.

Business Life from a Different Viewpoint

The Christian worldview is, at its very core, reality seen through the eyes of faith. Some people believe that faith is a mask that covers up a fundamental weakness. To them it symbolizes a deficiency, and they may even scoff at it. Faith from this perspective is blind. The truth, however, is that we are all compelled by our finite nature to walk by faith. The issue is not whether we live by faith, but in whom or in what we place our faith.

Our decisions always embody faith in something. We will ultimately make all decisions according to our faith. Those who do not seek Christ's will in business might develop their faith around highly personal independence, competition, material possessions, social status, or leisure. A Christian's faith, however, would place special value on the love and nurture of the family, the love of service, the health and well-being of the socially and economically disadvantaged, and the need to be kind and considerate of human differences. The Lord's day is also special to Christians, while many others see it only as another day to pursue commercial profits. This does not mean all Christians emphasize the same things, perceive the same risks, or respond to circumstances in the same way. We may have different priorities, emphases, and methods.

Those who do not love God do not associate going into business with fulfilling God's will for them. Christians, on the other hand, have an opportunity to see God's good intentions for them in a business career. Business is, after all, an institutionalization of God's intention for us to work and to serve each other. People form business organizations for a variety of personal, managerial, financial, legal, and other reasons; but Christians can see a much larger purpose in business. Business is a legal structuring of work where we express our dominion over creation. It affords us opportunities to plan, organize, lead, follow, and develop skills in a number of areas—all mirroring godly qualities.

Our culture alternates between applauding and condemning business. Many current public opinion polls reveal that corporate executives are not esteemed as highly today as they were some years ago. Some business people do not place moral principles very high in their decision criteria. Christians have a particular opportunity to be salt and light to the business world, and thereby demonstrate what it means to be ethical and moral.

Our way of life also places a strong emphasis on personal autonomy. Scripture affirms the value of the individual, but simultaneously calls each of us to understand that we are part of Christ's body. We are called to see ourselves as servants and stewards of something greater than ourselves. In this humble capacity we minister to others, while we are simultaneously ministered to. From a biblical perspective we are dependent, independent, and interdependent all at the same time.

The belief that God created us to be servants and stewards over his creation gives us a radically different view of business. If we have genuine faith in such understandings, we should exhibit our faith through our collective organizational behavior. The directors and managers of CMDS certainly took a faith position and expected it to influence their operations.

Some people would say that Christian faith is a "pie in the sky" view of reality and that it does not work in a world dominated by tough competition and selfish people. The faith described here, however, is neither wishful thinking nor abstract philosophy. And it certainly is not blind. Biblical faith is grounded on substantive, evidential facts: "Faith is the assurance [substance] of things hoped for, the conviction [evidence, proof] of things not seen" (Hebrews 11:1 NASB). God acts at specific times in history to communicate, demonstrate, and illustrate the way people are to live. The most relevant illustration is Jesus. He lived faithfully in a very tough situation.

This book emphasizes the faith characteristic of Christian life in business for a very good reason: because those of us who follow Christ are called upon to be different and act differently from those who have another object of faith. The distinctive character of Christian business professionals can come only through a commitment to Christ that is solidly grounded in an unshakable faith—an evidential faith.

Is Capitalism Christian?

"How is it possible for a person in America to be in business and still be a Christian?" That question was asked recently by a Soviet Christian to a visiting delegation of Canadian business-people. One was the president of a large furniture manufacturing firm. Another was a builder with a contract from the Soviet government to build a hotel in Leningrad. Another was the former president of a large real estate firm. All are deeply committed Christians active in local congregations and international Christian organizations. The Soviets found it difficult to see how a person in a capitalistic system—which emphasizes individual initiative, private ownership, competition, risk taking, and personal profit—could be a Christian. The Canadians were surprised because they couldn't understand how it was possible to be a Christian in a system that claimed to be atheist, emphasized government ownership of property, and limited personal freedoms.

Because business life is shaped by its political and economic environment, it is important to ask whether one economic system is more Christian than others. Both the Soviet Christian and the Canadian Christians assumed their system was best, and that it was easier to be a Christian in their system than in the other one.

The Bible was not written as a text outlining the best economic system, yet it does set criteria by which all systems should be judged. The following statements suggest some of the criteria that can be used to evaluate how well a given economic system serves the purposes God intended. Although these points do not relate directly to specific biblical passages, they do reflect the perspective of the Scripture taken as a whole.

1. The system should produce an adequate supply of products and services to enhance the quality of life.
2. The system should provide for the basic needs of marginal and disadvantaged people.
3. The system should respond to and allow for individual differences and needs. There should be fair and equitable means of resolving conflicts.
4. The system should reward and encourage initiative and hard work.

5. The system should provide meaningful work for all people and provide opportunities for them to contribute to the welfare of society.
6. The system should use natural and human resources efficiently and carefully.
7. The system should respect and care for other countries; it should not exploit them or rob future generations.
8. Power and access to power should be spread equitably among sectors of society and special interest groups.
9. The benefits of the system and the costs of providing them should be spread equitably throughout the system.
10. Human rights should be protected.
11. Individuals should be valued and given opportunity to grow and develop.

Christians can and should make judgments about the strengths and weaknesses of every economic system. However, in doing so, we must avoid labeling them as either Christian or non-Christian in any absolute sense. Every system has both positive and negative aspects. Systems work better at some times than at others. We should not become so attached to any one economic system that we overlook its weaknesses. No economic system is perfect. All need to be measured by the principles of Scripture.

No matter what economic system we participate in, we need to stop occasionally and marvel at the grace God has poured out upon all people in their business relationships. God blesses all of us with an orderly creation that can be developed for our benefit. The Holy Spirit regularly exercises moral influence to restrain sin and chaos in the economic arena. God endows all who bear his image with intellect and creative capacities. The talents associated with the work of a skilled machinist, competent truck driver, accurate accountant, reliable engineer, hard-working janitor, honest salesperson, discerning manager, or wise board member should be recognized as God's gifts to us. It is God's grace that gives gifts such as these even to those who do not acknowledge him as Lord.

QUESTIONS FOR REFLECTION

Corporate Goals

1. How do you respond to the statement of corporate goals at the beginning of the chapter?
2. Would these goals be appropriate for publicly held firms, or firms with many employees who are not Christian? What goals are appropriate for a Christian employee in a firm that makes no attempt to follow Christian ideals?
3. If you were a stockholder in CMDS, how would you feel about the statement on profits?

Exploring the Bible

1. Why does Jesus say in the story about the rich young man in Matthew 19:16–24 that it is "easier for a camel to go through the eye of a needle than for a rich man to enter the Kingdom of God?" Does this say anything about business?
2. Read Colossians 3:17. What does it mean to do business "in the name of the Lord Jesus"?

Contemporary Comment

1. In what ways do businesspeople compartmentalize their lives into sacred and secular sectors?
2. Many principles for working with people suggested in such books as *In Search of Excellence* are consistent with Christian principles. Is this surprising? Why or why not?
3. Can a Christian businessperson working with a kingdom perspective survive in the marketplace, where competition is tough and sometimes unscrupulous?

NOTES

1. CMDS Board of Directors, September 23, 1980. Used with permission.

Chapter 2

PERSONAL GOALS AND BUSINESS

What Do You Really Want?

A recent study of 209,000 college freshmen discovered that 75.6 percent listed "being very well off financially" as an essential or very important goal. Less than 40 percent listed "developing a meaningful philosophy of life."[1]

"This is what modern people have sadly concluded: Greed is the universal motive, sincerity is a pose, honesty is for chumps, altruism is selfishness with a neurotic twist, and morality is for kids, saints, and fools."[2]

And Conrad Black has said, "Greed has been severely underestimated and denigrated. There is nothing wrong with avarice as a motive, as long as it does not lead to antisocial conduct."

Defining Success

How do we measure success in business? Some people measure personal success by the position that they hold. By that definition, is a sales manager more successful than a salesperson? Others suggest that success is measured by the size of their paycheck or the amount of power they wield. Symbols of success such as titles, positions, wealth, influence, power, or status often have little to do with the real reasons Christians are in business: to do the will of God and to serve their neighbors.

We can climb the corporate ladder to positions of influence and acclaim for selfish reasons. It is true that successful people have opportunities that are not available to those who are less successful. Business success can provide the opportunity to live in the neighborhoods of your choice, own the type of car you like, send your children to the better schools. But success, increased power, and influential positions also open opportunities to serve. As a Christian studying business it is vitally important to identify what you really want. Are your aspirations for success similar to those college students in the survey quoted in the Point for Discussion? Or do they reflect the unique perspectives of your commitment to Jesus Christ?

Christians need to be very careful not to equate business success with God's special favor or God's approval. Just because a firm's profits are high does not mean that it is doing God's will or that it is meeting legitimate needs in its community. A successful dealer in illegal drugs, for example, is not likely to win God's approval for a successful business enterprise. One's personal income has little to say about one's relationship to God: God loves the person who fails in business just as much as the person who succeeds.

It is true that business success cannot be equated with righteousness, nor business failure with unrighteousness. But it is also true that when people live by scriptural principles, whether they are Christians or not, there is a greater probability they will prosper materially. Hard work will gain more than laziness. Honesty will build trust, which has a positive business side effect.

Because God both created and redeemed the world, the laws of nature and biblical wisdom are complementary. God's laws are not arbitrary. They really do reflect what is best for people.

The problem of equating God's blessing with wealth is sometimes called "prosperity theology." This way of thinking, which suggests that if we obey God he will prosper us materially, is false teaching. Prosperity theology perverts motives and reduces God to a vending machine provider of material wants. Such a view of God makes assumptions about his nature and character that do not square with biblical principles. Jesus came to forgive sinners, bless the poor, release the captives, heal the sick, encourage the downtrodden, and to perform many other saving works (John 1:29; Luke 4:16–21).

The unfolding of life under the care of our sovereign God is often beyond our comprehension. Scripture reminds us that "The mind of man plans his way, but the Lord directs his steps" (Proverbs 16:9 NASB). Job learned to trust God even when his material condition turned from success to desperation. We too must learn to trust God despite inexplicable differences in starting points and circumstances. There is no simplistic way for us to determine why one person is materially blessed and another is not. Hard work alone does not guarantee financial success; intelligence does not guarantee business success. We cannot predetermine the family we will be born into, nor the wealth we will inherit. We cannot know if the right idea will come at the right moment to be mixed with the right people and the right circumstances to generate business success. All of these uncontrollable factors influence how well we do in business.

Wealth, power, status, influence, rank, and other such symbols of secular success too often become substitutes for real success. Despite this there is nothing wrong with those kinds of success in and of themselves: it is the love of them that is so dangerous (1 Timothy 6:10). Christians do not necessarily need to feel guilty if they are financially rewarded or promoted to a higher-ranking position; but we must be careful not to fall in love with maintaining our own personal success.

The Genesis story portrays Abram as a very wealthy man. Yet, when there was strife between herdsmen of Abram and his nephew Lot, Abram did not first try to maintain his financial position. Instead he told Lot to choose—go left, go right, go to the valley, or stay in the mountains. Abram would take what was left (Genesis 13:5–18). Abram's conduct could have cost him a great deal materially; but he felt that unity, peace, and love were more important than his own personal success.

So how should Christians define success? The statements in the Point for Discussion, which endorse greed as a virtue and see financial success as more important than a well-developed philosophy of life, are certainly not consistent with a biblical perspective. God has told us to put first things first, to " . . . seek first his kingdom, and his righteousness . . ." (Matthew 6:33). His kingdom—his lordship in our lives—is what we are to seek.

Business success for Christians is defined in terms of service. It is not enough to look at the bottom line of the financial statement to determine how well a firm is doing. We must also look at such factors as how the firm treats its employees; whether or not it uses natural resources carefully; and whether or not the products it makes really lead to a better life for those who use them. On the personal level we should measure success in terms of how well we relate to others, how well we care for our families, and to what extent we are following God's will for our lives.

Some of us will be financially and professionally successful, with positions of power and influence. We will control wealth. Success, however, carries heavy responsibilities. A number of biblical teachings tell us that much is expected of those to whom much is given (Luke 12:48; Matthew 25:24–28; 1 Corinthians 4:2). Success, in a sense, is a take-home exam from God. Ultimately we will have to account to God for how we have managed our wealth, our talents, and our resources (Romans 14:12).

How Personal Goals Influence Behavior

Like light coming through a colored filter, our mental filter of reality—our worldview—dictates our behavior. If I have a self-centered, "me" orientation, I perceive life in simple terms: "What can I get out of it?" Unfortunately many people in business see people, things, and events in this way. They protect and advance their self-interest, even at the expense of others.

Certainly not everyone in business is totally selfish. Even people who have no interest in the concerns of God are quite capable of thinking of others. However, commitment to Jesus Christ dramatically reshapes and reforms our motives and drives. Christians do see the world in a unique way.

The personal drive for success shapes our behavior in subtle and not-so-subtle ways. Let's examine the following situation. Mary and Jennifer have both worked in the same department for several years and have become very good friends. They are talented women who have worked conscientiously at their jobs and have learned a lot. One day the department head is transferred, creating an opening for which both Jennifer and Mary are qualified, ready, and eager.

It is natural and right for people like Mary and Jennifer to want to gain promotions that will give them broader opportunities for increased responsibility and growth. Yet this same drive may become perverted and lead them to self-centered actions at the expense of the other person. They may use insincere flattery to ingratiate themselves with the person who will make the decision as to which one will be promoted. They may become jealous and nibble away at the reputation of the other by calling attention to faults or by starting false rumors. They may even do things to make the other look bad, such as slowing down work or withholding essential information. The competition for the promotion may become so intense that it fractures their friendship. These actions are quite consistent with a me-first orientation; they are inconsistent with biblical principles.

Imagine how differently they might act if they lived by Christian principles. They would try to maintain their friendship and build each other up rather than cut each other down. They would do their work in ways that make the other look good. They would be open and honest, not conniving and devious in their relations to others in the office. Each would compete assertively, but fairly, for the promotion. It certainly would be difficult for the one who did not get the promotion; but even then she would try to accept disappointment graciously and do everything she could to make the other succeed.

Personal goals can also influence important corporate strategy decisions. Corporate resources are sometimes used inappropriately to further the personal interests of individuals. Recently, for example, there has been an increase in the use of "golden parachutes." Golden parachutes guarantee large severance pay to top executives in the case of hostile takeovers, but make no provision for employees further down the corporate ladder. Sometimes top executives follow policies that increase their bonuses or short-term stock value at the expense of the long-term welfare of the company.

Recently, the executives of a stock brokerage firm paid themselves bonuses of $250,000 just before the firm declared bankruptcy. This meant that legitimate creditors were not paid. Some stockbrokers churn accounts in ways that increase their commissions, while their clients' portfolios decrease in value. Even some Christian evangelists divert contributions for their ministry toward their own lavish lifestyles. These are all examples of situations where selfish personal goals drive people to do things that are not ethical.

Businesspeople also seek capital funds on a competitive basis. Divisional managers compete with each other for a share of the capital budget. Top management's job is to weigh requests and to give priority to those that offer the greatest opportunity for a high rate of return. Behind this competition are individuals whose self-identity is closely tied to a need to appear successful. The budget figures that divisional managers submit may look exact, but they are merely projections or estimates. No intelligent manager will falsify such capital budget projections, but there are often subtle pressures to manipulate the figures. Managers may handle projected income figures optimistically, while expense and cost figures may be trimmed to unrealistically low levels—another example of business behavior shaped by personal goals.

God is not fooled by empty words, manipulated figures, or outward appearance. God knows our every motive, every thought, and every action. Christians are not immune from the temptations described above. But we are to "take captive every thought to make it obedient to Christ" (2 Corinthians 10:5). Christians must always ask,

- "Are the financial estimates I am submitting the most realistic ones?"
- "Have I subordinated my personal desires to Christ's will?"
- "Am I trusting the Lord to open and close the doors of opportunity for me, or am I manipulating events?"
- "Who am I serving, and in whom do I place my trust?"

We are called to serve Christ and, as empowered by him, to serve each other. We do not give our allegiance to God in order for him to assure us of worldly success. Our mental filters must not be "me first," but the filters of Scripture and service to Christ.

The Uses of Personal Wealth

Thoughts about money, how to get it, and what to do with it dominate many people's minds. Jesus talked about the dangers of becoming attached to money more than he talked about any other subject except the Kingdom of God. Money must be a very important subject.

How much of our material wealth should we use for personal enjoyment, and how much should we allocate for other purposes? One thing is for certain: the excesses we sometimes live out in the "American dream" are certainly *not* what God had in mind. The American dream says, "As people prosper, they are to increase their standard of living by purchasing more expensive homes, upgrading their automobiles, and traveling to distant and exotic places." Much of our spending is what Thorstein Veblen, in his famous book *The Theory of the Leisure Class*, called conspicuous consumption. This means we buy things not because they satisfy basic needs, but because buying and owning things impresses other people. The American dream is not the standard for Christian money management.

God calls us to be good stewards, not misers or ascetics. Self-denial is not an end in itself. "If I give all I possess to the poor . . . , but have not love, I gain nothing" (1 Corinthians 13:3). Paul says that delighting in self-abasement gives the appearance of wisdom, but is really a self-made religion (Colossians 2:18–23). Such self-denial is really self-serving. God does want us to live well. But the biblical perspective is that money is to be used to help the poor and build the kingdom, not to live lives of luxury nor to accumulate large sums of wealth.

The Bible also promises guidance for dealing with money.

But if any of you lacks wisdom [in the management of your wealth], let him ask of God, who gives to all men generously and without reproach, and it will be given to him. But let him ask in faith without any doubting . . . let the brother of humble circumstances glory in his high position [in Christ]; and let the rich man glory in his humiliation because like flowering grass he will pass away. (James 1:5–6, 9–10 NASB)

The person who has invested only in treasures on this earth is very poor indeed.

Money can come between us and God. Jesus looked the rich young ruler in the eye and told him to sell all his possessions, give them to the poor, and follow him (Luke 18:18–30). Christ knew what stood between this young man and God. The rich young ruler left sadly. He preferred to keep his money, even though it prevented him from following Jesus.

Money is not a neutral medium of exchange. Many of us only feel secure when we have money, and it has a powerful ability to demand loyalty and allegiance. As strange as it seems, people do worship money. They worship money when they measure their personal worth by how much money they have; or when they try to gain friends, status, acceptance, and respect by buying things; or when they flaunt their wealth. Trusting in anything or anyone other than God is idolatry.

It is important to examine our motives, to learn why we want to have and use money. If we look to money for security or prestige, it will make us slaves. We will never have enough. On the other hand, if we see money as a gift from God to serve others, we can use it for God's glory.

It is even dangerous to give with false motives. The stories in Acts 2:44 and 4:34–35 tell how people who had land and houses sold them and shared all they owned with the community of believers. Theirs was a beautiful, awe-inspiring, Spirit-generated love response. Acts 5, however, tells the story of Ananias and Sapphira. These two pretended to have the generous hearts spoken of in Acts 2 and 4, but they were selfish. They lied to the Holy Spirit by secretly keeping some proceeds from a property sale, while publicly declaring they had given the entire profit to the church. They were struck dead for their hypocrisy. The contrast is clearly a contrast in motives. Ananias and Sapphira's intentions were motivated by their desire to appear generous, not by a selfless concern for others.

Money cannot buy contentment. In September 1989 Leona Helmsley was convicted of income tax evasion. She owned many luxury hotels and was a millionaire many times over. Yet she treated her employees rudely, cheated on her taxes, and was ruthless in her desire for more money. Paul wrote to Timothy:

We have brought nothing into the world, so we cannot take anything out of it either. And if we have food and covering, with these we shall be content. But those who want to get rich fall into temptation . . . For the love of money is a root of all sorts of evil . . . But flee from these things, you man of God; and pursue after righteousness, godliness, faith, love, perseverance, and gentleness. (1 Timothy 6:7–11 NASB)

Paul also told the people in Philippi that he had "learned to be content in whatever circumstances" he found himself—whether with "humble means" or "in prosperity" (Philippians 4:11, 12 NASB). Our Christian contentment must be based on a faithful relationship to God and spirit-filled relationships with others.

God has also instructed us to give generously. The first tithe (giving 10 percent of income) recorded in Scripture is Genesis

14:17–24. This tithe was on the increase in Abel's wealth. It was a love response symbolizing thanks and trust, a grateful steward's response to the Master. The tithe later became the means of support for the Levites and priests. Yet the tithe is only our minimal response. Scripture often talks of tithe and offerings. Offerings go beyond the minimum tithe. Scripture also speaks of the gift of liberality (Romans 12:8 NASB). Giving freely and generously of our material blessings is a spiritual gift. Personal wealth should be used for giving to the church, as well as to local and global causes that are compatible with God's kingdom.

Some people today are promoting an idea called "first fruits giving." They suggest that each Christian, after careful study and personal budgeting, decide what percent of his or her income to give to the work of the Lord. The tithe is the minimum; many people find that by frugal living and careful management they can give much more. When each paycheck is received, the percent for the Lord is taken out and put into a special account. The rest is then used for normal living expenses and investment. This approach helps avoid the temptation to spend first, and then give from what is left.

One of the rich resources available to us to help us use money well is the community of believers, the church. God calls us to live our faith not in isolation as individuals, but in close relationship with other Christians. Community may happen in a local congregation or in a small fellowship group. Not many Christians discuss financial issues with others. A recent survey of Christian businesspeople in a small community indicated that fewer than 10 percent of them would feel free to discuss a financial problem with their pastors. Very few of us admit openly how much we earn. Our congregations and small fellowship groups can be very helpful.

For eleven years, the president of a steel fabricating company met regularly with a small group from his church for mutual support and direction. The group purposely included people with a range of incomes and job responsibilities. Because they all shared commitment to Jesus and represented various points of view, they were able to help and support each other in many areas, including financial decision making. By openly asking financial questions we can see where our own level of living fits in, and we can test whether or not given expenditures are necessary. Pastors can help us work through difficult ethical decisions.

Measuring God's Support in Lean Business Years

Christian businesspeople need to be on guard when thinking about God's blessings as they relate to the marketplace. Many people have a vague sense of divine checks and balances. It is easy for us to be tricked into thinking that when things go well we are living righteously and God is blessing us, and when things go badly we must be living in sin, and that God has abandoned us. This creates problems both when things are going well and when they are not. We have already seen that there is no perfect correlation between business success and the Lord's blessing. What about when business is failing or struggling? Is that a sign of God's wrath or neglect?

The Bible cites many examples of times when things went badly for good people. The obedient Israelites as well as the rebellious ones were taken into exile in Babylon (2 Chronicles 36:15–21). Daniel, Shadrach, Meshach, and Abednego were servants of God, and they suffered. Christ suffered on the cross and God loved him while letting him suffer (Isaiah 53). Both the rain and the sun fall on God's children, along with those who rebel against him. When Christians suffer they are tempted to conclude that God does not love them. But Scripture tells us otherwise. One of the paradoxes in Scripture is that Christians are promised suffering if they seek to live godly lives in Christ (2 Timothy 3:12). God has promised to use every event, even tough years in business, to build his children up in Christ (Romans 8:28).

Businesses get into trouble for many reasons, even when Christians run them. They may not have the newest technology to keep ahead of competition. Markets may change. We may be passed by for promotion because we lack the proper qualifications. We may not have the financial strength to expand our company as we would like, while some other firm with financial backing can move ahead. We make errors of judgment. Clearly lack of business success does not imply God's abandonment.

Just as we cannot equate business failure with God's judgment, neither can we equate business success with God's special favor. God blesses all of his people. We are blessed with eternal life and with forgiveness of sins. And we are blessed when we take on a worldview that is compatible with God's view. We are blessed when we are able to act justly and do what is right for our coworkers, our customers, our suppliers, and everyone else we serve. That is a blessed success.

QUESTIONS FOR REFLECTION

What Do You Really Want?

1. How do you respond to the quotations at the beginning of the chapter? Do they correspond with your experience?
2. One Christian businessperson suggests that Christians pursue positions of power, wealth, and success so that they can be "salt and light" in the financial and power centers of the world—missionaries to Wall Street. He said, "The world needs Christian tigers who can combine tough minds and warm hearts in such a way that they can be Christian, competent, competitive, caring—and successful."[3] What opportunities and risks are associated with this position?

Exploring the Bible

1. Read Mark 9:35 and Philippians 2:1–11. Both of these passages call Christians to be servants. What are ways we can be servants in business?
2. Read the story of the rich young man in Luke 18:18–30. What does this story suggest about goals for businesspeople? Why did he turn away?

Contemporary Comment

1. Make a list of your goals for the next several years. Be realistic and honest. List what you really want, not just what you think you should want. Discuss these with your friends. Compare them with the goals suggested in this chapter.

2. Do you agree with the point of view that "prosperity theology" is false teaching?

3. Make a list of principles that Christians can use to deal with personal failure in business. How can Christians help people who fail in business?

4. Under what circumstances might it be right for a Christian to declare bankruptcy?

NOTES

1. Alexander W. Astin et al., "The American Freshman: National Norms for Fall 1987" (Los Angeles: American Council on Education, University of California, Los Angeles, December 1987).
2. From an article decrying lying in American society. Walt Harrington, "Revenge of the Dupes," *Washington Post Magazine* (December 27, 1987).
3. Robert Gortner, "Needed: Christian Tigers," *Christianity Today* (April 5, 1985).

Chapter 3

WHAT DOES THE LORD GOD REQUIRE OF YOU?

Economic Justice for All

In 1986 the National Conference of Catholic Bishops published a pastoral letter called *Economic Justice For All*. They identified six key moral principles for a just economy.[1]

1. *Every economic decision and institution must be judged in light of whether it protects or undermines the dignity of the human person.* Economic perspectives must be shaped by three questions: What does the economy do for people? How do people participate in it? How can the economy serve people and not the other way around?

2. *Human dignity can be realized and protected only in community.* The obligation to "love our neighbor" has an individual dimension, but it also requires a broader social commitment to the common good.

3. *All people have a right to participate in the economy.* It is wrong for a person or group to be unfairly excluded or unable to participate or contribute to the economy.

4. *All members of society have a special obligation to the poor and vulnerable.* As followers of Christ, we are chal-

lenged to care for the needs of the poor, to speak for the voiceless, and to defend the defenseless.

5. *Human rights are the minimum conditions for life in community.* Human rights include not only political and civil rights, but the right to food, clothing, shelter, rest, medical care, education, and employment.

6. *Society as a whole, acting through public and private institutions, has the moral responsibility to enhance dignity and protect human rights.* Private institutions, the church, and the government have an essential responsibility in this area.

What Does the Lord Require?

Everybody agrees that it is good to love our neighbors. Yet translating that love into specific situations takes a lot of effort. The larger Christian community has spent too little time addressing the question, "How do I love my neighbor in business?" The answer to that question says a lot about what God requires of Christian executives, Christian supervisors, Christian salespeople, and of all Christians. The organizing principle for determining how God would have us apply love in business is contained in this passage: "He has told you, O man, what is good; and what does the Lord require of you but to do justice, to love kindness, and to walk humbly with your God?" (Micah 6:8 NASB).

God issues a clear call to his followers to do justice, love kindness, and walk humbly with him. This verse helps us focus in fresh ways on a command so familiar that we often only consider it superficially: the command to love our neighbor.

Doing Justice in Business

Imagine that you are a Christian entrepreneur who develops a business manufacturing chemicals for industrial coatings. Demand is increasing. There is great potential for growth. But the work is dirty and unpleasant. It requires little skill and is repetitive and boring. Mishandling raw materials or finished products can lead to serious injury and, perhaps, permanent disability.

Luckily you've stumbled onto a source of eager workers: Cambodian refugees. They're grateful for any job, they work hard, and they demand little beyond a paycheck. So you hire twenty-five of them at minimum wage. But as your business grows, your conscience asks a nagging question: "What does it mean to do justice to these employees in my business?"

Doing justice is a major theme of Scripture. It is referred to hundreds of times as either an obligation of God's people or as a promise to be fulfilled. Justice reflects God's character, which he wishes us to embody and reflect. Justice is a complex word that embraces the relationships that should exist between people.

When we talk about justice our minds usually turn to thoughts of civil and criminal justice, where restitution or compensation are required to right a wrong. While that is one type of justice, it is not the most common type talked about in the Bible. Biblical justice refers to the ways relationships are structured so that there are no built-in disadvantages to any individual or group of people. Many of the Old Testament prophets rebuked the Israelites precisely because they had not practiced justice in the marketplace. They treated people and groups of people unfairly. The biblical command to do justice is a call to righteousness; it is a call to do the right thing in the right manner with the right motive. In your role as an industrial coating entrepreneur, you might ask yourself about your motives for hiring an immigrant work force, your methods of hiring them, and your treatment of them as employees. These are all questions of justice in daily business decision making.

One of the ways biblical justice is expressed is through the covenants God has established with people. Justice was part of a continuing commitment and relationship that God maintained regardless of the unfaithfulness of people. God expected loyalty and service; but he was faithful even when the Israelites disappointed him. When hiring refugees for the industrial coating business, as in all contracts and relationships, biblical justice requires faithfulness that goes beyond the bare terms of a contract. The idea of covenant modeled after God's covenant is helpful. Max DePree, former president of Herman Miller, Inc., a manufacturer of fine office furniture, talks of covenantal relationships rather than contractual relationships.

An article in *Fortune* describes these relationships.

At the heart of Herman Miller's management system are what Max DePree calls covenantal relationships between top management and all employees. He defines the company's central mission as "attempting to share values, ideals, goals, respect for each person, the process of our work together." In contrast, he says, many companies settle for contractual relationships, which he says "deal only with precedent and status."[2]

Biblical justice is characterized by a deep concern for the well-being of the poor, who are often oppressed and exploited. In the Bible this concern is extended to widows, orphans, and strangers. God is deeply concerned for the people on the bottom of the economic ladder. The Catholic bishops address this concern in the Point for Discussion. Their propositions clearly describe Christian obligations to meet the material needs of the poor and vulnerable.

People at all levels of business must treat each other fairly and without prejudice. They must together work to build structures that protect the rights of everyone and take care of the weakest people. Justice involves doing an honest day's work as well as paying fair wages. The emphasis here, however, is on those in positions of authority. Because they have power, they have a special responsibility to practice justice. But what does this mean? How are we as Christian business professionals to embody justice in the workplace?

One specific decision area is compensation. Christians should not be content to meet only the minimal requirements by funding the "going wage," required workers' compensation, and mandatory retirement programs. These are determined by law and by market forces. As Christians we should be driven by a love for doing what is just and right and not simply accept the legal and market answers.

We cannot ignore the market, but we can make choices regarding wages, prices, costs, expenses, and other economic factors, where there is room for discretion.

Think how you would go beyond the minimum legal requirements to express justice if you were the industrial coating entrepreneur. You might use the resources of your firm to provide language classes for your employees; or you might take into account living costs in your area as you set wages. You might provide bilingual people in your personnel department to be sure that the concerns of the refugees can be heard. Although none of these things are required, in the long run they are good for business because they will help develop a competent and loyal work force. In the short run, of course, such measures are costly. When business is bad it may not be possible to go beyond the minimum. But even then it is necessary to be fair.

People in management exercise considerable judgment when making decisions that allocate profit. Values and priorities influence these decisions more than market forces do. Important decisions such as how to divide profits between hourly wages, salaried compensation, bonus and profit-sharing programs, earnings retained and reinvested, and dividends need to be made from the perspective of justice. Justice requires that workers as well as managers and owners benefit when firms are profitable.

If you were the manager of the industrial coating company you would also need to decide how much difference there is between lower- and upper-level employees in wages and perks. Sometimes local wage scales are lower than national ones. Is it just to go with the lower one? Historically jobs traditionally held by women have paid less than similar jobs held by men. The low pay scales for nursing, teaching, and secretarial work are examples. In spite of the fact that it is very difficult to determine whether different jobs are comparable in skill, justice requires serious efforts to pay comparable wages for comparable work.

Doing justice in the marketplace means there is an honest relationship between the quality of products and their prices. Isaiah

1:22 talks about the sin of those who diluted the wine and mixed waste matter with their silver. God is concerned with the quality of the product related to its price. God is concerned with the intent that rests behind our decisions. If we charge more for our products simply because the market will bear it, we have not carefully considered all the factors that determine a just price.

Christians who intend to do justice must also pay attention to their employees' working conditions. The Catholic bishops argue for environments, both physical and psychological, that protect human dignity. We are responsible for the safety of every work environment whether it is a slaughterhouse, a machine shop, or an office building. The personal environment includes relationships with supervisors, subordinates, and peers. These too must be "life giving" and not demeaning. For example, we cannot allow ourselves or those we supervise to tease people insensitively or to use derogatory language. Such lack of empathy creates a hostile and therefore unjust environment.

Finally, doing justice involves opening the doors of opportunity, within the bounds of our authority, to any person capable of accomplishing the required tasks. This requires special efforts to tear down barriers from the past that have discriminated against women and minority groups. Christians have responsibilities to go as far as they can to assist people who are capable of growing sufficiently to be competent in the jobs they seek to fill. If we desire to be just, we make efforts to train those who are handicapped, deprived, inexperienced, or new to our country.

The need for justice in business should continually touch our Christian consciences. Our decisions about wages, prices, safety standards, recruiting policies, and a host of other issues must mirror our concern for doing the right thing in the right manner with the right motive.

Is Doing Justice Too Expensive?

Doing justice is not cheap. A nurse who worked with AIDS patients contracted the disease in the course of her work. Businesses are facing high costs in providing elevators and other means of access to physically handicapped persons. Opening the doors of opportunity to groups that have experienced discrimination in the past requires special training programs and other readjustments of established patterns. This means money.

When we see injustices in our places of work, we need to respond in ways that promote justice. Often there is no easy answer. For example, suppose your workers are exposed to toxic chemicals that could cause significant health problems in later life. No cheap solution is available. In fact doing justice is so costly that the firm loses its competitive edge.

There are many ways to avoid facing such issues. Some managers simply wait for the government to solve the dilemma through regulations. Others rationalize that the whole issue is simply too big and complex, and therefore unsolvable. Some companies choose to pay insurance premiums to protect themselves rather than try to correct the problem. Some companies fight government regulation. Other companies, in an effort to maintain fair competition, have taken a more positive approach and have asked for industry regulation so that all companies face the same costs.

The first step is to recognize that those responsible for the oversight of a company or job are also responsible for the well-being of those performing the tasks. The next step is to believe that something ought to be done. We should not accept injustice as necessary just because of competitive or market conditions. To do this is to become slaves of the market. Such behavior is wrong. Injustices must be redressed.

Consider the dilemma of nurses who face daily stress working in the emergency room of a hospital. Their problem can be addressed in a number of creative ways. Additional pay might help compensate. Psychological tests could be used to identify personality types capable of better tolerating job-related stress. We could offer special training and technological assistance. We could limit the number of continuous weeks a nurse may work in this environment.

We need to be very wise when we meet resistance to our efforts to establish justice in the marketplace. We cannot expect easy success just by identifying problem areas. Nor can we expect others to quickly respond to Christian principles.

We can certainly appeal to prudence, the ability to exercise good judgment in practical matters, as a universal ground. Prudence suggests that it makes good sense to reduce the risk of lawsuits, government regulation, escalating health costs, and other identifiable potential problems. While we go beyond prudence to act from love, it is often helpful to demonstrate the prudence of actions to those who do not have the higher motivations. The appeal to prudence is more limited in scope than Christian love, but it does not contradict it.

Christians in business are obligated to seek justice, but we are free to seek it in a way that makes sense to those not motivated by Christ's interests. The wise person "makes knowledge acceptable" to everyone (Proverbs 15:2 NASB).

For example, a Christian could suggest to management that a system be developed so hospital employees feel free to report perceived problems in emergency room procedure or management to an ombudsman. Such a procedure would elevate morale, increase loyalty, reduce turnover, and raise productivity. The person making such a suggestion is simultaneously seeking to improve the quality of justice in the workplace and making good business sense.

Can we always afford to redress an injustice? Our answer must be yes. We simply cannot afford not to. We should not be naive in saying this, though. It will take time and money in most complex situations, and we will frequently meet with resistance when costs are involved. It will probably take hard work. And, while there is no guarantee that we will be successful in eliminating the injustices, our responsibility is to try and try and try (Ezekiel 3:16–21).

Loving Kindness in Business

Kindness is the support that must accompany justice. Justice focuses on what we do; kindness focuses on how we do it. The call to love kindness is a reminder to Christ's followers that our lives are not only to be characterized by righteousness, but our relationships are to be characterized by kindness. We are to be friendly, empathic, gentle, generous of spirit, tenderhearted, and merciful. Our kindness is to reflect a personally directed, heartfelt concern for the well-being of our neighbors.

Kindness does not depend on external circumstances or one's personality. Difficult as well as pleasant situations all need to be handled in a kindly manner. It is easy to love those who are naturally lovable. Even people who do not follow Christ are able to do this. The challenge is to love persons who are habitually late for work, inadequately performing on the job, creating peer competition and tensions, or who have grating personalities.

Addressing and correcting inadequate performance is a frequent responsibility in business. It is an easy task to compliment a proficient worker during a performance evaluation session; it is more difficult to correct an employee's inadequate performance. Occasionally we come across a supervisor or manager who seems to enjoy letting people know when they are deficient in some way. Such managers rarely execute the task with kindness. Another supervisor may keep silent about underachievement and wait until the next economic downturn to let a worker go, on the grounds of hard times. That is both dishonest and unkind.

Love demands that inadequate performance be addressed kindly. Although we must never attack human worth, dignity, or value, we must never fail to confront unacceptable behavior and performance. To be just and kind is to seek positive, corrective action and carry it out in a manner that demonstrates and affirms the value of the worker while constructively communicating the need for change.

A conversation with an employee who has been having problems might go something like this: "Jack, you and I have had four discussions in the past three months about your performance, and Bill [Jack's supervisor, who is sitting in on this meeting] tells me the rejection rate on the welds you perform is still running twice the allowable tolerance. You certainly can't take any satisfaction in that. It isn't kind of us or wise for you to remain in a job requiring specific skills that are just not present. Neither of us could feel good about that over the long haul.

"I would like you to read this letter that will be placed in your file. It speaks highly of you in every way pertaining to your character, attitude, and cooperation. It notes the single skill deficiency as the cause for letting you go from this department. Bill will go down with you to the personnel office, and they are prepared to help you with tests to determine if a skill-job match can be found and to assist you in locating another job in our plant, or with another employer if that becomes necessary. Take advantage of their help. That is what they are there for. I am truly sorry to let you go, for you possess the very qualities of integrity and hard work we like around here. I hope you will be satisfactorily relocated very soon."

Kindness never implies weakness. Kindness does not close its eyes to reality. Kindness does not skirt hard circumstances. But it is upbuilding. It understands and acts with compassion. It is gentle and supportive in the situation.

Walking Humbly in Business

Justice and kindness focus on what we do in business and how we do it. The third requirement of Micah 6:8, walking humbly with God, addresses the spirit in which justice and kindness are carried out.

Humility lays the foundation for the first two—do justice, love kindness. Humility comes from knowing the character of God and understanding our need of God. We need mercy; God extends it; we become merciful. We need patience; God is patient; we become patient. And on it goes, so that we learn to extend to others the love that we so richly receive from God. Humility is a product of a proper focus on God's mercy in Christ and a close personal relationship with Christ.

Humbling ourselves is foundational for developing the servant attitude to which we are called. False pride, an inappropriately elevated opinion of ourselves, occasionally raises its sinful head in the life of every one of us. Part of our call to take up the cross daily and follow Christ is to do battle with the "elevated self."

We do not develop humility by comparing ourselves with other people. Downward comparisons develop false pride. The sales rep with the best performance record does not grow in humility by comparing himself with the one with the least sales. Furthermore, the maintenance of such pride requires many defenses that inhibit true love and godly service. Humility has few, if any, self-defenses, and thus sets us free to care for others and elevate them to positions of genuine significance. For example, one of my sales representatives makes a poor presentation to the product task force. Do I, as a sales manager, embarrass her by taking over the floor and demonstrating my superior knowledge by explaining it myself? Or do I recall publicly the strengths of her presentation and talk privately of her weaknesses? Events like this should be handled humbly, with loving concern.

Upward comparisons, on the other hand, can generate self-pity. The typist who averages two errors while typing sixty-five words per minute doesn't develop healthy humility by noticing the person at the next station who types eighty-five words per minute and averages one mistake. Such self-pity only makes us and others feel unwanted or overlooked when the promotion to office manager goes to someone else. False pride is not true humility, but neither is self-pity.

Humility comes from a right understanding of the answer called for by Paul's question to the Corinthians, "What do you have that you did not receive?" (1 Corinthians 4:7). Why should any of us boast of our talents and gifts? They were given. To be unkind to those less talented than ourselves or envious of those more talented than ourselves is, in the final analysis, to find fault with God. Instead we should praise God for the gifts he gives each person and turn them toward service.

What does it mean to walk humbly with God in business? It means daily recognizing our dependence on God, graciously accepting the gifts and talents God has given us, and using those gifts and talents to serve others. An inappropriately elevated or deflated self does not help us serve customers or employees in the proper spirit. Only when we walk humbly will we treat customers and employees kindly and do justice by them.

QUESTIONS FOR REFLECTION

Economic Justice for All

1. Can you identify important aspects of economic justice that are not included in the statement at the beginning of the chapter?

2. In what ways do you agree and what ways disagree with statement 4, which suggests that all members of society have a special obligation to the poor?

3. What differences and similarities are there between this statement and the conditions that are actually found in society?

Exploring the Bible

1. The Hebrew word for peace is *shalom*, which means to be whole, sound, safe. It describes the world as God would like it to be. The following passages suggest aspects of shalom: Isaiah 66:12; Psalms 41:12; Genesis 26:26–33; Psalms 82:30. Identify these aspects.

2. In the New Testament the word that captures the idea of the world as God wants it to be is "kingdom." Read the following passages: Luke 1:46–55; Luke 4:18–19; Matthew 5–7.

Contemporary Comment

1. What is the relationship between just social and economic structures and personal well-being? How can Christians in business work toward just structures?

2. How does the approach in this chapter reinforce or contradict other approaches to business that you have heard?

3. Are there times when kindness and mercy in the short term might not be so in the long term?

4. Use the following case to discuss the issues of justice, kindness, and mercy. How are each of these applied?

For fifteen years Lisa worked as a secretary for a Christian organization. Over the years she had worked hard and was loyal to the organization. Most of the time her work was adequate, but she did not do as much as others at her level. Sometimes others needed to do more than their share because she did less.

The organization did not have a good system for evaluating her performance but it was able to work with her because it was doing well financially. Her boss was kind and patient, and he complimented Lisa often. He did not want to be unkind, so he did not criticize her poor performance. Her coworkers were frustrated, but Lisa felt that she was doing well.

Then several things happened at once. The organization began to experience financial difficulties, so staff needed to be reduced. The older department director retired and a new one was hired. He saw at once that Lisa was not performing adequately. In addition, this department was merged with another one so that the workload increased significantly. Lisa was not able to adjust to the increased workload.

The new department head feels strongly that Lisa should be let go. He comes to you for counsel. What do you recommend?

NOTES

1. Adapted from *Economic Justice For All* (Washington, DC: National Conference of Catholic Bishops, 1986): ix–xi.
2. Kenneth Labich, "Hot Company, Warm Culture," *Fortune* (February 27, 1989): 74–78.

Chapter 4

REAL PEOPLE: A BIBLICAL UNDERSTANDING OF HUMAN NATURE

POINT FOR DISCUSSION

Cookies and People

Everyone likes chocolate chip cookies, be they soft chewy ones or firm crispy ones, with huge gooey chunks of chocolate that melt in your mouth. This year Americans will spend more than $500 million on over-the-counter chocolate chip cookies.

In the July 1984 issue of *Inc.* magazine, Tom Richman compares two of the leaders in this market, Mrs. Fields Cookies and David's Cookies. In addition to different opinions about what makes a good cookie, the owners, David Liederman and Debbie Fields, have very different approaches to working with people. Notice how their assumptions influence how they manage. The point is not that one is right and the other wrong, but that each approach seems to work in its own setting.

David Liederman tries to minimize the number of people involved. He automates as much of the process as possible. Cookie dough is made in a centralized plant. All the employee must do is put the dough on a baking tray, put the tray in an automatic oven, and collect the cookies 7 1/2 minutes later. He says he is "terrified to send anything out there where an employee has to do anything to the food . . . You have to think in the lowest common denominator."

Mr. Liederman says, "The realities of the retail business in any typical urban environment are not wonderful: the external robberies, the internal robberies, the motivation. You're dealing with kids who really are just passing through. The kids are the 'Achilles heel' of retailing." He quotes a friend in another business who says, "My job is to keep my employees stealing as little as possible."

Mrs. Fields, in contrast, doesn't mix dough in a central plant. Instead, store employees combine ingredients (some in proportioned containers) that are shipped to the store by independent distributors. Ovens are not automatic. Employees must put the raw dough in the oven and judge when to take the finished cookies out.

"Mrs. Fields Cookies," says Debbie Fields, "is an extension of how I see the world. I believe people will do their very best, I really do, provided that they are getting proper support . . . You say that people come to work for the money, and I disagree with that. Money is part of a whole picture. People come to work because they need to be productive. They need to feel like they are successful in whatever they do . . . Money is not the issue."

Mrs. Fields and David's represent two rather different approaches to the management of people. Both companies are very successful and have expanded rapidly in recent years.[1]

Capable Image Bearers

Every business operates with assumptions about human nature. Debbie Fields believes that people need to feel productive and successful. David Liederman believes employee commitment is limited. There is evidence to support either assumption. What should we as Christians believe about the nature of people at work? What concepts will guide our management style?

A familiar Christian belief is that we are all created in the image of God. We believe this is critical to our thinking about people on the production line, in the office, or at the board of directors meeting. This is a foundational truth that should permeate our thinking, for it is at the core of what it means to be a human.

What does it really mean to be made in the image of God? On the one hand, it means that we are creatures in relationship to our God. All that we are comes from God. The Apostle Paul tells us that. Christians are being renovated and restored to the image of God when the Holy Spirit gives us a true knowledge of God (Colossians 3:10), which radically alters our view of life and the world; we are being renovated in righteousness; and we are being renovated in holiness (Ephesians 4:23–24). We were created to know God and have God's view of reality; in knowing God we can come to know and do what is right in his sight; and in knowing God and doing right we can separate ourselves from evil and be holy. As Christians we are being renovated to the likeness of God and are called to devote ourselves to God's interests.

On the other hand, the concept of image bearing applies to those who do not recognize their need for a unique relationship with God. Whether people are Christians or not, they are still authentic image bearers. Those who reject God's renovating work remain separated from God and pursue their own desires. They are not motivated to serve God or to seek his will, even when they do things that serve and benefit others. Like broken mirrors, these images are distorted. Yet everyone has the same fundamental worth, value, and dignity because we have been created in the image of God.

The Genesis account of creation provides us with a clear picture of human nature as God intended it. First, God gave us special status in the world. Although God cares for all of his world, he is especially concerned about us. We are to be treated with dignity and respect no matter what our level of ability. We have intrinsic value. That means we are important just because we are created in the image of God. Our worth is determined by who we are, not by what we do.

Second, God delegated to us authority to make decisions that really matter. We are not merely puppets on the end of a string. Our choices make a difference for us and for all succeeding generations. For example, God has given us responsibility to care for the environment. If we burn holes in the ozone layer we may well create environmental changes that will make life very difficult for our children.

Third, because God needs fellowship, we do too. We are created to live in community. Our economic system and business itself are social institutions created by people who lived before us. We inherited these structures, but we have the power to change them because we were created in the image of God.

Our memory, ability to reason, desire to plan, power to conceptualize, ability to act, capacity to be constructive, urge to create, skill to build, capacity to make moral judgments, and all our other abilities are marks of our having been created in the image of God. God expects us to organize our work in ways that build on and develop those characteristics. We glorify God when we strive to reach the potential God has given us. Business professionals have a special obligation to encourage human development, for most adults spend the greatest proportion of their waking hours working. In that regard Debbie Fields is right in her desire to help employees be productive in their work. Every human talent is created by God. There is no justification for its waste.

The Shattered Image

God looked at creation and said it was good. It was perfect: justice, kindness, and love governed relationships, and there was harmony. But Adam and Eve chose to sin. Their sin affects all who now choose to reject God and the patterns of relationship God suggested. This has enormous consequences. Just think what it would be like if everyone were honest, as God intended. We wouldn't need to lock our cars or houses. We would not need to spend money on jails. Businesses would not need to spend money to protect themselves from shoplifters. Customers could know that advertisements gave honest information and that product claims were true.

The fact that Adam and Eve and every one of us since then has chosen to sin dramatically shapes the way we do business. Sin is not only personal; it has become rooted in our organizations and ways of thinking. Much of what we do is oriented toward recovering from and controlling its effects.

We would like to be able to work with people and assume that they always want to do what is right and that they are motivated to be creative and do good work. But that is often not the case. In the real world we must compensate for the fact that sin has caused the image of God in our lives to become shattered. Our motives are not always pure. We sometimes need threats to make us work up to our potential. We are too often ready to settle for mediocrity rather than excellence. We are not always trustworthy. In this regard, David Liederman's assumptions about people are correct.

We must recognize that temptation is everywhere in business. When we place people in positions of potential temptation—handling large sums of cash, overseeing valuable merchandise, being under great pressure in a job where cheating will probably escape detection, and so on—we must also provide controls over that temptation. Then we need to explain clearly why we have controls to help us exercise self-control, and what those controls are. Prior knowledge of possible temptations and an effective plan to eliminate the temptation are the two best defenses against immoral behavior. In this regard we have a responsibility to be our brother's keeper in business.

We must take sin seriously in the business environment and find ways to use both positive and negative rewards to help people control their behavior.

Positive Rewards and Negative Consequences

Three forces form a moral magnetic field and help keep us on a positive course of behavior: love or commitment to internal moral standards; positive rewards for good behavior; and negative consequences for inappropriate behavior. If any of the three ceases to function, enormous pressure is placed on the others.

There is no force as powerful in guiding human conduct as love. When people love deeply they project that love in thought and action. Paul expressed this idea when he said, "The love of Christ controls us . . ." (2 Corinthians 5:14 NASB). Christians know this reality and can accrue a double set of positive rewards from work. We can enjoy the positive results of our work; but we also see that our work is part of God's total plan to bring eternal life (Matthew 19:29; John 3:16). The recognition of this eternal dimension gives courage when we are faced with hardships like the loss of a job, illness, or broken relationships at work. We enjoy the peace that comes from a forgiven and clear conscience and the fellowship of God through his Spirit and the Scripture. We have the special council of God for all situations and circumstances in life. Our work has purpose and meaning; we have the joy of pleasing God. And these are only a sample of our positive rewards!

Those who do not love Christ do not have the love of Christ to control them, but they may still have an internalized commitment to high moral standards. Through family upbringing, social reinforcement, or other supportive means these people derive a significant portion of their self-identity through maintaining a moral standard. Those commitments undergird strong moral conduct in the business community.

Both the response of love shown by Christians and the commitment to moral behavior maintained by others are commitments that spring from within. They are internal commitments, although they do have different origins. This internal commitment to love and the standards that relate to it is the first force in the moral magnetic field pulling people toward good behavior.

The second force is the pull of positive rewards. These may be spiritual in character, but often are not. Many rewards are tangible: money, power, prestige, promotions. One management consultant suggested that people would work long and hard to get their name on a parking space because of the prestige associated with a private parking place. Other rewards, like personal fulfillment and the satisfaction that comes from doing a job well, are less measurable. These rewards can be used to encourage quality work. We can, for example, provide bonuses to employees who report safety problems in the plant.

We are taught and come to enjoy the positive aspects associated with good work in many ways. As children we learn the connection between good conduct and rewards—chores related to allowance, praise related to good grades, and so on. Athletic training and learning to play by the rules of the game also reinforce the positive conduct–rewards connection. We carry these lessons right on through life and into business. We often subconsciously perform as good team members within the rules because we know it leads to the best outcomes for us.

Many people are turned on by the rewards associated with performing well in business. Some see business as a giant game and respond to rewards of winning. Many see it as an avenue for creative self-expression. People do not all derive the same rewards from work, but most have a relatively positive view of its rewards. Given the availability of such rewards, most people will respond by performing well.

The third force that helps to keep us in a positive path of moral conduct is the presence of negative consequences for inappropriate behavior. We know it is not wise to throw rocks at a hornet's nest or neglect our studies before a test. Similarly we understand that we should follow business policy if we wish to avoid censure or dismissal. Excessive absenteeism can lead to termination. Lax follow-up on customer warranties could lead to demotion. We must never entirely put out of our minds the specter of negative consequences, even though we are called to lead positive lives. The prospect of negative reinforcement comes to our aid whenever temptations or bad habits must be overcome.

Responses to Inappropriate Behavior

Managers need to learn to deal with inappropriate behavior in a positive way. Few of us naturally come by the skills required to do justice and love kindness. We must usually struggle to develop such skills.

Only the naive would fail to guard against and act to eliminate the overt consequences of our fallen nature. We are all subject to immaturity, the development of bad habits, errors of judgment, troublesome desires, self-centered conduct, a presumptuous attitude, fatigue, and a host of other human conditions that lead to inappropriate conduct. These traits reflect our fallen nature. Employers don't train their employees—intentionally, anyway—to do what is wrong, but many hours are spent in correcting and training them to do what is right.

Inappropriate behavior, whatever the cause, is hurtful on two levels. Those who behave inappropriately waste their human potential, and they create negative consequences for those around them. As an employer or supervisor you should follow these five important steps when correcting inappropriate behavior.

1. *Genuine concern must accompany your desire to eliminate the undesirable consequences of poor conduct.* Successful reproof of another rests on three ingredients: a previously established caring relationship between the parties, wherever possible; a genuine interest in the person at the time of the correction; and the certainty that it is the conduct or behavior of the person that is being addressed, not his or her personal worth. Say, "I'm concerned about the unusual number of billing errors you've made lately. Can you explain the problem to me?" That's much better than, "Can't you get anything right? These bills are all wrong."

2. *Clear communication regarding expectations must always precede corrective action.* Any discussion of inappropriate behavior implies a standard of behavior. Did the offending party know what standard was being applied and what was expected? Punitive consequences should be administered only when the affected party could have reasonably anticipated the action. The bottom line is simply this: tell people what is expected and the rewards and consequences associated with the expectation. If your expectation is that a billing mistake should occur in only one of every one hundred bills sent, tell your billing clerk that on orientation day.

3. *Never simplistically assume that directives regarding work expectations and consequences have been clearly understood.* Genuine care carries with it the responsibility of making certain your message is understood. This requires feedback. Can the person being addressed repeat and explain—indicating understanding—the message? Does your billing clerk understand why a low error rate is critical in your company?

4. *Administer positive corrective action as soon as possible following the offense.* Waiting allows the offense to be repeated, fosters the perception that the behavior will be tolerated, and dulls the memory of the event to the point that it is forgotten or becomes unclear. Don't wait until you have a list of all the billing mistakes for the past six months. Discuss them when they occur.

5. *Correction must be fair.* Fairness encompasses such considerations as: Was the correction done in private so as not to be unduly embarrassing? Would others have been disciplined for the same offense? Could the consequence have been reasonably anticipated? Was the individual personally attacked or was it conduct that was corrected? Lack of fairness will do more to obstruct the desired positive response than anything else. If you put pressure on this clerk to make fewer mistakes, you can't ignore the errors of the shipping and receiving clerk.

Along with our obligation to address inappropriate behavior we have a responsibility to eliminate or reduce obvious temptations. Temptations are awakened desires whose satisfaction would be immoral. Although there are no limits to the variety of human desires stimulated in the work environment, we can reduce the level of temptation by carefully designed control structures and make consequences commensurate with offenses.

Christians can successfully appeal to high standards of morality and justice in the marketplace on the basis of prudence. Everyone will agree that the production of high-quality products will build customer loyalty and benefit long-term profitability. We can also promote the idea of obeying all federal and state laws on the grounds that being careful promotes public trust and avoids fines. In the same vein, supporting the needs of employees reduces personnel turnover. Those who do not seek God's ways are not ignorant; they can be asked to do right because it is prudent.

Christians have a worldview that differs from others, but Christians cannot claim to have greater technological or intellectual competency. We must nurture the abilities of those who are not Christians with the same respect and dedication that we would want for ourselves, for all people bear God's image. Christians acknowledge that everyone has a fallen nature, but we know that everyone also carries the authentic image of God.

QUESTIONS FOR REFLECTION

Cookies and People

1. These companies have very different assumptions about people. List the differences.
2. For which company would you like to work? Why?
3. Which company would you guess gives the highest return on investment? (Both are privately held, so that information is not open to the public.)

4. Is one approach more Christian than the other? Can Christians be tough? Defend your answer.
5. Identify ethical issues related to the use of automation.

Exploring the Bible

1. We are made in the image of God (Genesis 1:26–27; 9:6). How does this affect the way we relate to people in business?
2. People are both *finite*, which means their knowledge is limited, and *fallen*, which means they choose to do wrong things (Psalms 51:5). How do both of these factors affect how you will work with people?

Contemporary Comment

1. Robert Merton, a sociologist, wrote about "self-fulfilling prophecy." He suggested that if people think something is true they will act as if it were true and it will often become true. For example, if a student thinks a class will be boring, he or she will act as if it is boring and it will be boring. How does this apply to working with people? Refer to the Point for Discussion at the beginning of this chapter.
2. Christians often work closely with people who are not Christians. Sometimes they even share business ownership. How does this affect how they might work with people?

NOTES

1. Tom Richman, "A Tale of Two Companies," *Inc.* (July 1984): 38–43. Reprinted with permission, *Inc.* magazine (July 1984). Copyright © 1984 by Goldhirsh Group, Inc., 38 Commercial Wharf, Boston, MA 02110.

Chapter 5

HUMAN IDENTITY: IN THE WORLD, OR IN CHRIST?

Identity

At every moment you choose yourself. But do you choose *your* self? Body and soul contain a thousand possibilities out of which you can build many I's. But in only one of them is there a congruence of the elector and the elected. Only one— which you will never find until you have excluded all those superficial and fleeting possibilities of being and doing with which you toy, out of curiosity or wonder or greed, and which hinder you from casting anchor in the experience of the mystery of life, and the consciousness of the talent entrusted to you which is your I.

—DAG HAMMARSKJÖLD[1]

Therefore, if anyone is in Christ, he is a new creation; the old has gone, the new has come!

—2 CORINTHIANS 5:17

Sources of Identity

If you were asked to identify yourself in one hundred words or less, what would you say? Would others who know you well write a similar description? Is your identity attached to people? Things? Roles you play? Is there a difference between who you would like to be and who you are? Do you ever find yourself in roles for which you are not suited? Would others who know you well write a similar description?

Sometimes the gap between the person we would like to be and the person we really are is quite wide. This gives room for growth, but it can also create serious problems in business. In his book *The Peter Principle* Dr. Laurence J. Peter suggests that many people are promoted through the organizational ranks until they end up in positions that are over their heads. They are unhappy because they do not have the capacity to meet the new challenges. Many other people land in jobs which they do not fit. Either their supervisors did not know them, or they did not know themselves.

This gap can be created by pressures to be what we are not. For example, a child can be told throughout his childhood that he is going to be a wonderful medical doctor like his father and grandfather, only to discover years later that his natural aptitude is not in biology and chemistry, but in art or music.

If we do not know ourselves we may overstep our capacities or fail to use gifts that we have. If we do not truly understand others we will place them in situations where they cannot succeed. Our identity is not static. In a real sense, we work all of our lives to discover ourselves.

Those of us in Christ are having our true identity restored with the help of the Holy Spirit. In *Biblical Concepts for Christian Counseling: A Case for Integrating Psychology and Theology* Dr. William Kirwan ties our psychological identity to our faith in Christ. He suggests that we are undergoing an identity transplant as the source of our identity is transferred from the world to Christ.

As this identity transfer is taking place, we need to grasp Christ's perception of us so we will be encouraged to continue to grow in Christlikeness. To know Christ is to become like Christ (1 John 4:15). Those who do not identify with Christ maintain other sources of identity and often misinterpret their identity in some significant ways. This misinterpretation can affect their ability to be effective in their work life.

Psychiatrist Abraham Maslow identified the relationship between basic human needs and identity. He theorized that there is a need hierarchy. One builds from the foundation of physiological needs for food, water, and shelter; up through a hierarchy of safety needs, social needs, and esteem needs; to self-actualization needs. He believed that realizing one's greatest potential self-expression was the highest level of need fulfillment. Self-identity is directly tied to one's place on the hierarchy. People at subsistence levels would define themselves around activities of gathering food. Those at higher levels would tend to define themselves in terms of esteem and self-actualization.

God created us with a number of inherent needs—physical, psychological, spiritual—and provided means for their satisfaction. Because we live in a sinful world, we will not reach perfect satisfaction. We will examine three central psychological needs that are common to everybody: the need for unconditional acceptance, the need to be competent, and the need to belong. We will look at how personal identity and business behavior are deeply influenced by the quest to satisfy these basic needs.

Acceptance

Our need for unconditional acceptance springs from the very core of our being. It is tragic that so many of us accept a counterfeit in its place. This counterfeit is conditional acceptance. We experienced acceptance only when we got the right grades in school, wore the right clothes, or joined the right club. If we have not experienced unconditional acceptance before entering business, we will arrive with a deficiency that will indelibly shape our professional conduct.

We need unconditional acceptance. In business we are hired for our knowledge, skills, potential, and performance. This is only fair. Yet we still need to be accepted simply because of who we are.

While we consciously or unconsciously seek acceptance to reassure ourselves of our worth, we become subject to a myriad of external influences. In business we're not so different from teenagers who typically do many things they otherwise would not do to gain acceptance from their peers. When we enter business with this need for acceptance unsatisfied, we are particularly vulnerable to overt or implied calls for any behavior that we believe will merit acceptance.

A great deal of unethical behavior begins under the false rationalization that the particular action will gain a favorable response from the organization. Cost accountants in defense industries know that simple screws should not cost several dollars apiece. Product designers may know when O-rings are being produced too fast to insure top quality. Hardly a month goes by without some business-related scandal making the news. Those involved in such incidents know their conduct is wrong. But, as ethicists have known for thousands of years, there is no inherent necessary correlation between knowing what is right and doing what is right. Why? Aren't businesspeople rational? Yes, but sometimes only to the degree that it reinforces their self-identity. When being rational fails to reinforce our unmet need for acceptance, we begin to rationalize the inappropriate conduct we feel is necessary to enhance our identity.

All of us need to be accepted not only for what we do but for who we are. God unconditionally accepts all who are in Christ. His acceptance is not conditioned on any work that we might do. It is a free gift, a gift of grace.

In return we are to be a positive force in demonstrating such Christlike unconditional acceptance in business. Our interest in people must extend far beyond our relationship to them as economic producers. We can model unconditional acceptance by doing and saying things that show genuine respect for the worth, value, and dignity of all individuals, regardless of what they know and do.

People who come to work deficient in their need for unconditional love may be self-protective and defensive about their work. Brent will continuously explain why defects in the chairs he upholstered were never his fault, but always the fault of the raw materials, his coworkers, interruptions, or outdated machinery. Only if Brent feels unconditional acceptance will he be able to take responsibility for his mistakes.

Workers might also cover up their lack of acceptance by attempts to overachieve. Joanne may not take enough time with her family in the morning because she always wants to be the first one in the office, impressing coworkers with her early morning energy. Both defensive and driven people can relax if they know they are accepted for who they are. It is the task of managers to accept people this way.

Competence

God also created us to be competent. We need to express what we know and to demonstrate our ability to act competently. This is fundamental to our sense of well-being. Our search for success is generally channeled through constructive activities as we work hard to purchase the homes, cars, vacations, educations, and other things that symbolize competence.

Sometimes the need to be competent and successful drives people to be unethical. Ivan Boesky was convicted in 1987 for insider trading. He was portrayed in the public press as being obsessed with making money.

Mr. Boesky possessed amazing intelligence. He was a talented entrepreneur. His education was of the highest caliber. What went wrong? Boesky's own public statements point to a compulsive, driven personality with identity needs so strong that he was unable to exercise self-control. His need for superior competence in his field of investor arbitrage drove him beyond legal limits.

As Christians we have particular resources for dealing with the need for competence in our own lives. We define "success" as following the will of God. This makes us less susceptible to the temptations to compare ourselves competitively with others. It also means we have the resources of other Christians to help us keep a clear sense of perspective.

We must help others find a sense of competence in their work. We must pay attention to the careful selection, orientation, training, appraisal, and development of employees to help them find a place where their skills fit organizational needs. Placing a person in the wrong job with inadequate orientation will undercut his or her sense of competence. Failing to help train a new coworker in proper procedures encourages failure. Developing the competence of others requires close, careful, and regular attention to the people with whom we work.

Belonging

The third need everybody seeks to satisfy is the need to be a member of a group. This differs from the need for unconditional individual acceptance, which depends on others for its satisfaction. It reveals our need to serve within a group while receiving what is necessary to make us a whole person.

Americans do not generally associate their need to belong and its satisfaction with belonging to a business organization as the Japanese do. We tend to think of the family, church, civic club, or some other social unit as places to experience belonging. Much has been written recently about Japanese companies and their family characteristics. Many Japanese seem to satisfy their basic need to belong by identifying with their business organizations. In that context many social and recreational needs are also met. Their job is often a lifetime commitment.

American industry can learn from the Japanese. As industry faces heightened foreign trade pressures there are more accounts in the business press of companies reducing their labor force through early retirement, attrition, transfers, and voluntary separations. The anxiety and even anger this causes reflect not only an economic threat, but also a sense of organizational betrayal. The reciprocal commitment and loyalty that once were traditional are now being torn apart.

For Christians, the church can become a primary community centered on a commitment to Jesus Christ where they find belonging. Emphases among Christians vary. Some denominations believe that it is within the community of believers that God disperses his gifts, and that apart from this community one is not able to grow nor to experience the fullness of Christ. In addition, strong emphasis is placed on the community as a larger family where concrete, caring action is taken in times of financial need, sickness, natural disaster, birth, death, and special building projects that affect one family or the entire fellowship. Christians can find support for ethical decision making in these small groups. Other Christian denominations emphasize only church attendance, personal devotions, and relatively autonomous personal ministry. These Christians live their lives relatively free from involvement in a larger fellowship.

The majority of Christians participate in a church fellowship that falls somewhere between the "church as community" and the "church as a voluntary option." However, our commitments in life and our identity are definitely affected by the model of the church we pursue. Our ideas about the life of the church community will influence our lives profoundly. We participate in God's family as a primary source of our belonging. Most of us would be greatly enriched by increased participation in a local congregation.

We all need to see ourselves in business as well as part of an ongoing team working together. We should not, for example, take our decisions to hire or fire an employee lightly. When employees are hired they join a community of people at work, and many workers will desire to stay with this group for a long time. We should be sure that the job we offer provides for long-term possibilities. If it doesn't, perhaps it's better to hire from a temporary agency whose workers have few long-term expectations. When we release someone we should similarly be sure our reasons are good ones. Isolating any person from the community of workers is a serious issue.

Authentic Identity and Behavior

Why do people so often do what they know is wrong?

People do what they do to gain acceptance, demonstrate their competence, and to be part of a social group where they can give and receive. The drive to satisfy these desires is basic, and occasionally overrides what people know rationally is the right thing to do. Self-justifying rationalizations are often used to justify actions that people think will gain acceptance, competence, or belonging.

What will rule our lives in business? Where will our cues come from? It is perfectly clear that God does not want us to develop our identity from position, wealth, power, or prestige. God wants us to have a genuine identity in Jesus Christ, not a counterfeit one.

If anyone would come after me, he must deny himself and take up his cross and follow me. For whoever wants to save his life will lose it, but whoever loses his life for me will find it. What good will it be for a man if he gains the whole world, yet forfeits his soul? Or what can a man give in exchange for his soul? (Matthew 16:24–26)

Christ's requirements are radical when contrasted with the world's. The world speaks of self-actualization. Christ calls us to die to self, daily. Acceptance cannot be realized by doing something that tarnishes the image of God in ourselves or others. We should not attempt to show how important we think we are by bragging or flaunting our competence. We understand that all we have is God's gift to use to serve his will.

QUESTIONS FOR REFLECTION

Identity

1. What might Hammarskjöld mean by suggesting that there is only one "I" in which there is "congruence of the elector and the elected"?
2. List some of the superficial ways businesspersons may try to find identity.

Exploring the Bible

1. Study some of the passages in the Bible that include the phrase "in Christ" (such as Romans 8:1; 2 Corinthians 5:17; Galatians 3:28; Philippians 2:5 ff.; 1 Thessalonians 1:3). What do these suggest about identity?
2. One translation of Romans 12:3 suggests that Christians should have a "sane estimate of their own capabilities." Is it appropriate to acknowledge that we have skills and abilities? When does that acknowledgment become pride?

Contemporary Comment

1. Examine your own identity. Who are you? What factors have made you who you are? How does your commitment to Christ affect your identity? You might want to write a short autobiography to answer these questions.
2. We form identity through modeling. Do you know some businesspeople who model a Christ-centered identity?
3. Entrepreneurs need a high level of self-confidence and ego strength. How does this fit with the Bible message to "deny one's self"?
4. One of the primary forces that helps form our identity is our choice of friends and associates. Where can businesspeople find supportive, understanding, Christian groups with whom they can discuss business issues?

5. What can Christian managers do in the workplace to encourage acceptance of people for who they are rather than for what they do?

6. How can people who really like their work avoid finding their identity only in their work or in the products they produce?

NOTES

1. Dag Hammarskjöld, *Markings* (New York: Alfred A. Knopf, 1965), 19.

PART 2

Work: God's Intention and Our Response

Chapter 6

DOING JUSTICE IN THE WORKPLACE

A Furniture Design Company Considers Justice

"We have had a participative management process at Herman Miller for more than thirty-five years—long before participative management came into style. We define participation as the opportunity and the responsibility each employee-owner has to be included in the decision-making process to the level of one's competence and job responsibility.

Participation is not permissive. It requires competence, discipline, and commitment. We believe participation enables us to achieve above-average results. Douglas McGregor once said, 'We cannot force people to work for management's objectives.' But through participation we can improve personal commitment to business results.

At Herman Miller, ownership is more than just psychological. One hundred percent of our full-time regular employees with one or more years of service in the United States are stockholders. When this program was introduced in 1983, Max DePree [then CEO of Herman Miller, Inc.] said, 'I believe it is significant that all employees in the company are stockholders because it is synergistic with the participative management process which we have had since 1950.' Max went on to say that employee stock ownership is a clearly competitive reality—nothing is being given. Ownership is earned and paid for through the Herman Miller profit sharing plan, which has been in place since 1970.

"There are three values connected with business ownership: literacy, equity, and spirit. To fully carry out our responsibilities as owners, we must be literate in our business. We expect a knowledgeable, professional team of people who understand the values, goals and operation of our business. For participative owners, this means the responsibility to understand our role and the role of others in the company and to seek clarity when it is not apparent. And it is the right to be informed of the true situation with respect to our company and jobs.

Our value of equity means that we strive to achieve an equitable return for our customers, employee-owners, and investors. For participative owners, this means we must work with justice and a sense of fairness. It also means we have the opportunity to share in the results (whether positive or negative) of our work. We expect the sharing to result in both financial rewards and psychic rewards.

"A third value related to ownership is spirit. We value excitement, enthusiasm and energy at Herman Miller and expect people to have a positive attitude. We believe in the importance of celebration and tradition. For employee-owners, this means we share commitments to the company, its goals and to each other.

"Our Herman Miller values can be summarized in just six words: innovation and excellence through participative ownership."[1]

Fostering Justice

Herman Miller Corporation believes that justice is fostered by spirited sharing of employee ideas in an open, equitable, participatory environment. So do we. Christians are to be stewards of ideas. The development of ideas can be planned and is predictable. We cannot force others to generate specific ideas, but we can provide an environment like the one at Herman Miller that looks for, stimulates, and rewards creative suggestions.

We are by nature thinkers and problem solvers. For example, a student, asked to do a term paper in macroeconomics, wants to examine the problem of inflation. After making a list of possible approaches, she narrows the topic down to the central bank's role in fighting inflation. Then her mental wheels begin generating ideas about specific problems and alternative solutions. These same desires to zero in on a problem and begin to solve it also work in business decision making. They apply for people who are concerned with market and product research, production flow and efficiency, quality control, accounting reconciliations, and personnel selection. All business problems need to be solved by stimulated human minds.

To develop such needed creativity we need to believe that our ideas are wanted and valued. Christian managers must consider it their responsibility to develop work environments that foster the creation and utilization of constructive ideas. This enhances the worker's stature, brings enormous benefits to everyone, and also brings glory to God.

Justice and its accompanying openness to ideas embodies the fullest concept of loving your neighbor and of being truly concerned for the best interests of others. It builds on the question and answer of Micah 6:8. "What does the Lord God require of you?" The requirement is to do justice, to love kindness, and to walk humbly with God. Let's examine a few areas of business in which participation and equity will foster justice and human creativity.

The Significance of Work

The story is told of a tourist in Europe who, on his way to see the tourist attractions, passed a stonemason working beside the walk. For several days the tourist observed the mason chipping away at the stone. Finally she stopped and asked why he continued at such boring and repetitive work. The man replied as he pointed to the unfinished cathedral high above his head, "To you it may look as if I am chipping away at a stone. But what I am really doing is building that cathedral."

Justice in business requires that we help every worker understand the significance of his or her work by showing how it contributes to a larger task. The copy editor is really contributing to the spread of important ideas. The receptionist contributes to the feelings people have about the firm by answering the phone in a pleasant voice. The groundskeepers at a college contribute to the mission of the college by creating a beautiful environment. People need to find for themselves how they contribute to the finished product. Managers can help all employees feel part of the whole.

Francis Schaeffer, a twentieth-century Christian theologian, wrote *No Little People* to make the point that every person and every job is significant. Karl Marx, a nineteenth-century atheist, argued with enormous energy that capitalism is evil, precisely because he believed it separated people from a holistic work experience.

It is true that some jobs carry greater responsibilities than others. Responsibility may be greater according to numbers: number of people we supervise, number of products we make, number of budgeted dollars we allocate. Responsibility may also be higher on a scale of critical importance: the person who decides when the chocolate has been stirred enough at the chocolate factory has more responsibility than the person who cleans the chocolate vats. Yet that doesn't mean that jobs supervising fewer people or making smaller product decisions don't matter. All jobs are significant because of what they contribute to the whole of the business.

Consider the gardeners at the plant who cut the grass and trim the shrubs. Think about the production workers who work all day at a knitting machine making socks. Can they find genuine significance in their work? When we compare these tasks with the responsibility of setting a product's price, or of making a final decision on a plant expansion, they may not seem very important; but their contribution to the whole is significant. These workers are significant precisely because their jobs do contribute to the accomplishment of the overall goals of the business. They are, therefore, exercising their responsibilities before God.

Yet, beyond the recognition of everyone's contribution, doing justice in business carries an obligation to provide opportunities for employees to exercise as much responsibility as possible. For example, the people who cut the lawn could also be asked to develop a comprehensive lawn care program. That would enrich their responsibilities. Responsibilities for the routine maintenance of their equipment could also be assigned to them to broaden their range of tasks. These groundskeepers could also be allowed to participate in decisions regarding the replacement or upgrading of equipment. The people sitting at the knitting machines making socks can be asked to think about ways to improve the efficiency of their operation. They might be capable, in some cases, of offering beneficial machine design suggestions. Opportunities to participate in such problem-solving need to be provided. Production workers could probably offer helpful suggestions for ways to reduce boredom and fatigue.

We need to ask, "What will make these people's work more creative and responsible? What tasks will use their ideas as well as their physical efforts?" We have an obligation to find and implement answers to such questions. Why? We could reduce costs and increase productivity. That's good business. But the gains in the quality of life for those involved are even more important. Human dignity is enhanced.

Providing a Quality Work Environment

Doing justice in the workplace also has enormous implications for the quality of the work environment. When we talk about the work environment, we should think of everything from health and safety matters to office decor. Our environment is made up of everything that surrounds us at work: surfaces people walk and work on, lighting, noise from people and equipment, privacy and openness, size of the work space and its arrangement, and so on.

That quality is influenced by government standards. We should implement and internally enforce all government requirements regarding the work environment that do not contradict God's explicit commands. The Christian has no moral defense for the willful violation of public law. If the standards are unrealistic or unnecessary in the judgment of those who implement them, every effort should be made to change them through the appropriate channels. In the meantime every reasonable effort should be made to comply.

We should go beyond minimum government standards to provide a quality work environment. This includes giving careful attention to health and safety needs.

Whenever possible work environments should be attractive and pleasant. Even in manufacturing plants a lot can be done with paint and light. Good design, quality art, and carefully selected colors can help relieve stress and improve morale and productivity. The issue of justice enters when there are significant gaps in the treatment of different workers in the same business.

Quality of the work environment always involves relative judgments. We tend to evaluate our own conditions by comparing them to the condition of others. Some people are absolutely destitute, and others relatively poor. The same must be said for the rich. Many people are relatively wealthy. For example, a family making $60,000 a year with two children in college and a home mortgage in northern New Jersey does not, in all probability, consider itself to be wealthy. Yet to a young neighbor seven blocks east who is making $30,000 a year and raising four small children, the other family is definitely wealthy! It's all relative.

Those relative comparisons are part of judgments of working conditions. Are there significant differences in the working conditions of those in executive suites, those in lower positions at the corporate headquarters, those in the plant offices, and those on the factory floor? Compare the condition, privacy, and cleanliness of the different restrooms. If there are recreational and health facilities, who has access to them? When people go to eat, do the facilities differ between those in the lower and upper echelons?

Some differences are appropriate. Good carpeting, for example, is not appropriate for the floor of a foundry. But unjustified differences in luxury do raise the issues of justice. They may create great psychological distance between different levels of employees. They can cause an executive to view her newly redecorated office with more telephone lines as a status symbol to show her superiority over others. Vast differences in conditions may even communicate the belief that some employees are much more valued than others. It is easy for those reaping the benefits to rationalize and justify preferential treatment between levels of workers and managers, ascribing ascending levels of importance to those up the ladder. Instead we need to be salt and light as we seek equity in working conditions as an important part of seeking justice in the work environment.

Expressing Justice Through Compensation

The concept of relative equity also affects our decisions about just compensation. Apart from obeying civil law, there is no absolute standard by which doing justice in compensation can be measured. God calls upon us to do justice by paying just wages: ". . . I will draw near to you for judgment, and I will be a swift witness . . . against those who oppress the wage earner in his wages. . ." (Malachi 3:5 NASB). How, then, can we determine whether or not a compensation program is just?

Let's develop an answer by looking at the concept of equity and the results of a market-driven economy. Is equity (not equality) within a job class a necessary component of a just wage and salary structure? If our answer is no, we conclude that what person A gets paid is unrelated as a matter of justice to what person B gets paid. If, on the other hand, we answer yes, then all wages and benefits in the company are related to each other on the premise that justice inherently relates one wage decision to a standard for all similar decisions. If this is true, then person A's salary must necessarily be seen in the light of person B's salary. That addresses our concern for compensation fairness within a job class.

Yet if a just wage for a given job class must be an equitable wage, how can we determine the "standard wage" or referenced wage for a job class? When goods and services are sold in a relatively free economy there are two possible answers. One answer assumes that the market is fair and just. This suggests that the person be paid the going market rate. If we assume the market rate is just, we have paid a fair wage. Or we could start with the market value of our goods and services and work backwards through our expenses and costs (materials, capital, labor, and management). After we decide internally on what is available, we could then decide what is equitable for everyone. In the first case the market sets the standard wage, and in the second case the wage is set by determining what is available and equitable.

Christians living in a market economy must ask whether the market is just in all cases. The market sets wages and compensation through an informal bidding process, governed by labor supply and demand. There are many good things about the way the market sorts through the allocation of labor resources. The market is so broad and deep that it generally keeps individual managers and companies from gross manipulation of the wages they pay. If a company wants to fill the skilled position of welder or customer service representative, there is a known market range of wages. If wage rates are too low, a skilled worker will look for better alternatives. If wage rates are reasonable, the company can hire a decent employee. If wages get too high, driving up product costs, competitors can provide customers with a cheaper alternative. The market when it works well protects the individual, the company, and the consumer.

There are, however, several morally disturbing aspects of using the market process alone to determine the wages of different job classes. The market sometimes reflects specific cultural values that cannot be justified in the light of Scripture. Discrimination based on gender is one such example. At one organization highly skilled administrative secretaries are paid at a lower rate than poorly trained people in jobs with lower skill levels in the maintenance department. The administrative assistants are generally women. The maintenance department personnel are men. Some studies show that even with increased efforts to pay men and women at comparable rates, there is still a significant discrepancy.

In a highly competitive environment the market wage set for a whole class of workers may fall below wages acceptable to support the needs of employees. Wages in one-company towns are generally lower than in towns where there is competition. Suppose your company is the only major employer left in a town that has been hit with plant closures. The labor supply is abundant. People cannot easily move away because of investments in houses and because of family and community attachments. You could hire for minimal wages. But would doing so be just if those wages are below what it takes to support a family? The market would push you to minimize costs and keep wages low. The biblical concern that wages adequately support a household should be a serious consideration.

The last problem—equity associated with the spread between the top and bottom of pay scales in business—is a difficult one, but it warrants careful consideration. The average American top executive makes ten times as much as the average laborer. In many firms the differential is even larger. The absolute figure of "ten times as much" doesn't prove an injustice, but it does call our attention to the equity issue. One church educational organization, recognizing the importance of this equity issue, established a rule of thumb that the highest-paid person in their organization should receive no more than five or six times what the lowest-paid receive. The lower wage levels are a bit higher than comparable ones in the community. The higher levels are considerably lower than comparable ones. In similar organizations the ratio often extends to fifteen times. They have addressed the issue concretely, though probably not perfectly.

The compensation package of most top corporate executives is made up of a base salary, stock options, and a variety of other profit-sharing incentives and perks. Let's assume all this is absolutely just. The equity principle requires us to ask if the typical laborer, in the same corporation, is afforded stock option plans and profit-sharing opportunities. Are the systems of pay equitable? Do they provide the same opportunities? If the systems are not equitable, there is little likelihood that compensation will be equitable.

But, it can be argued, since managers carry higher levels of responsibility and risk, don't they deserve higher compensation? The owner of a small business who risks her life savings and home to invest in a business and who works long hours in the early stages to get it started does deserve more from the business because of that risk and effort than her employee, who works an eight-to-five day. It is also true that people deserve a fair return for capital investments they make in business. But what about equity? At one point in the history of Chrysler Corporation the workers took a rollback in wages to allow the company to work through some difficult times. The president, Lee Iacocca, announced rather broadly that he would accept a salary of only one dollar that year. Several years later, when the employees were still working for the rolled-back wages, Mr. Iacocca received a large bonus and salary of several million dollars. The unions threatened to strike for higher wages because of the inequity they experienced. Chrysler gave in because of this pressure.

The Point for Discussion suggests that leaders at Herman Miller, Inc., work very seriously at the issue of equity. They believe that all employees should share broadly in the financial as well as the social and psychological rewards of their work.

We cannot be faithful in doing justice in a compensation system unless we ask these hard questions. This does not imply that the market system is a bad system. It does imply, however, that it is an imperfect system and not the only factor that needs to be considered in setting compensation. In general we will be guided by the market system, but we will take steps to move toward more equitable distribution. Christians need to be sensitive to equity issues and try to develop systems that foster equity. We are called to "do justice" in the marketplace. Everyone should have an equitable opportunity to share the good and bad results of effort.

QUESTIONS FOR REFLECTION

A *Furniture Design Company Considers Justice*

1. How does Herman Miller, Inc., help employees feel that their jobs are significant to the company?
2. Do you agree with Herman Miller, Inc., that justice in compensation requires an employee profit-sharing plan and employee stock ownership? Why or why not?

Exploring the Bible

1. Read Matthew 25:14–30. Based on this parable, whose responsibility is it to develop the "talents" of workers? Does the owner in this parable offer any encouragement to those who use their talents? How does this passage relate to the production worker sitting at a sock-knitting machine all day?
2. Read James 2:1–7. What do these verses say about creating a better environment for those of higher position?
3. Read Matthew 20:1–16. Do the results in this parable seem equitable from our perspective? Is this a parable about equity in wages and the power of the employer?

Contemporary Comment

1. Think about a personal work situation where you were treated unjustly. How did you react?

2. Nissan Motor Manufacturing Corporation, USA, opened its Smyrna, Tennessee, plant in the early 1980s. The usual executive perks, like special garages and dining rooms, were not installed. All employees who want to eat in the plant do so in one of two cafeterias, and parking is first-come, first-served. The plant is also equipped with basketball hoops and fifty ping-pong tables. There's a swimming pool and a planned family recreation center. Does this company's plan seem compatible with ideas about justice explored in this chapter?

3. Compare the pay of professional athletes and rock musicians to that of teachers and secretaries. Why do these differences exist? Is that unjust?

4. Ben and Jerry's Homemade, Inc., is a Vermont-based maker of premium ice cream. Its 1987 Stockholder's Report states that corporate policy is to pay its highest-paid employee a base salary no more than five times the base salary of the company's lowest-paid full-time employee. Says Ben Cohen, one of the owners, "No one deserves to make the kind of money big business people make." What are the advantages and disadvantages of such a policy? How should Christians weigh these pros and cons?

NOTES

1. Excerpts from *Business as Unusual*. Used by permission of Herman Miller, Inc. Copyright © 1986 Hugh DePree, quoting Richard Ruch, chief executive officer of Herman Miller, Inc., Zeeland, MI, 129–30.

Chapter 7

JUSTICE AND THE OPPORTUNITY TO WORK

Work Is a Healing Process

One of our company customs is to have an appreciation dinner for people who retire. Some time ago, a man with a congenital hip problem retired. He has walked with a severe limp all his life. At the dinner we were sitting next to each other. I asked him, "Arthur, do you have pain all the time?"
"Yes, I do."
"How many years have you had this pain?"
"All my life—for sixty-five years."
"How could you work with all that pain?" I asked him.
He put his hand on my shoulder. "The trouble with you healthy people is that you don't realize that work is a healing process."[1]

Everyone Deserves to Work

Isn't it going a bit too far to suggest, as the Point for Discussion does, that work is a healing process? Most of us would do anything we can to avoid work. Or would we? One of the really difficult things about being sick is that we cannot work. Even children get bored after several days' vacation from school because they do not have work to do.

When Adam and Eve were created God gave them the responsibility to take care of the garden (Genesis 2:15). They were given authority over all the animals. Work is a natural and important part of life. It is through work that we are creative and that we produce products or provide services that benefit ourselves and others. The ability to work is a gift from God. God worked in creating the world. Because we are created in God's image, we find meaning and fulfillment in work too.

There are many kinds of work. Some are organized and provide salary; other work is volunteer, such as with the United Way or the church. Some kinds of work, like cooking and yard work, come because we are part of families. Some work is honored and publicly acclaimed; other work, such as caring for an invalid grandparent, often goes unnoticed.

Access to meaningful work is a fundamental consideration of economic justice because work is so central to our purpose in the world. Salaried work is also the primary means in our society for getting the money we need to live.

In ancient Israel there were three ways in which people were given access to productive capacity. In that agrarian society land was the most important resource. First, the land was divided between the tribes by lot (Numbers 26:55–56; 33:54; Joshua 13–19). Not everyone got exactly the same amount or quality. The tribe of Dan, for example, got one of the smallest inheritances, but was the second largest group. And Manasseh, who was to get a double share, ended up with approximately six times as much land as his brother Ephraim's tribe. The tribes were not equal in their starting points.

Within each tribe those with greater need were given greater resources. The families within the individual tribes were to divide the land so that the larger families in each tribe would get more land than the smaller families (Numbers 26:53–54; 33:54). Within the families of each tribe there was a principle of equality at work.

The Jubilee principle was established to rearrange access to resources and the work associated with them. Every fifty years all land was to revert to the original holder's family so that no family would be permanently disinherited or refused access to the means of production (Leviticus 25:15-41). This principle meant that poor judgment, material inequalities, or misconduct of one generation would not have perpetually negative effects on subsequent family generations. Despite initial inequalities, God wanted everyone in Israel to work and have access to productive resources.

There is probably no greater dehumanizing force in the world than structures that deny employment, for whatever reason, to those who want to work and are able to do so; or structures that prohibit certain groups of people from gaining promotions or from moving into upper levels of responsibility.

We will specifically address four kinds of discrimination that affect our society: race, sex, physical disability, and age.

Racial Discrimination

All societies have some kinds of racial discrimination. Until very recently South Africa had a system of job reservation that reserved jobs beyond specified levels for white people. A black person could get a job in an automobile repair shop doing menial work and handing tools to the mechanic as long as he worked under the direction of a white person. But no matter how much experience he had or how much he knew, he could not get a job that required supervising others or total responsibility for the job.

Our society has no laws that foster discrimination in this blatant way, but many subtle forces lead to similar results. De facto discrimination places artificial impediments to job access or promotion. It gives one group advantages God never intended. It is a contrived system that makes some groups superior to others.

Racial discrimination has been a major barrier to employment opportunities over the centuries. Majority and powerful groups have found some way to exploit minority groups whenever there were ways to distinguish between the groups. Sometimes discrimination is based on color, such as when whites discriminate against blacks. Sometimes discrimination is based on physical differences, such as between Europeans and Asians. Heritage, religion, and ethnicity were factors in the Nazi discrimination against Jews.

The problems created by discrimination continue long after the direct practice is changed. Slavery has been illegal in this country for more than a century. There have been laws for several decades against job discrimination based on race. Yet the effects of earlier discrimination remain.

Families who years ago were not able to enter college cannot pass on to their children the attitudes and advantages they missed. People forced to live in poverty because of housing and job discrimination experience structural forces that prevent them from developing skills, habits, and attitudes that help them get good education and jobs.

The Bible is clear on two points regarding reparation for past wrongs. Those individuals who are responsible for injury are to be held personally accountable for making restitution, and those who suffer a definable loss are due payment (Exodus 22:1–15). Also, nations and groups of people who discriminate incur long-term costs of such discrimination. South Africa is experiencing severe economic difficulties because of its failure to use the resources of the black population. There is continual political instability and fear among the whites because of the unjust policies.

As a part of their contribution to society businesses must find ways both to eliminate current discriminatory practices and to catch up for past wrongs. God wants everyone to have meaningful and productive work and to have access to productive resources. We should be leading the charge to hire a diverse multicultural work force.

Sex Discrimination

Sex discrimination also limits opportunities for women and, to a lesser extent, men. Some policies discriminate against single people. Some years ago a Christian organization provided benefits such as medical insurance to men on its staff, but not to married women—because they assumed the women would receive those benefits through their husbands! That kind of blatant discrimination is no longer legal, and it was certainly never right.

Both men and women are created to enjoy the gift of meaningful and productive work (Genesis 1:26–27). Proverbs 31:10–31 describes a very successful and industrious married woman. She was something of a superwoman, who probably had a number of servants to help get everything done. In the agrarian society of biblical times women worked beside their husbands. In the Bible God gave many commands to correct role stereotypes that had developed. The stereotype would have suggested that women had primary responsibility for children. Yet God gave fathers special responsibilities for educating children. The need for fathers to love their children was given special attention by John the Baptist when he called the fathers of his day back to a loving care for their children (Luke 1:17). It was not assumed that fathers should place their career ahead of their love for their children. Both mothers and fathers must wrestle with the tensions that can build up as they seek to balance God's creation mandates regarding family, work, and worship, and as they break out of the role stereotypes of the past.

The Bible really takes a very revolutionary stance for the culture in which it was written. It portrays godly women in a variety of work situations that defy tradition. The church at Corinth included Lydia, a seller of purple-dyed cloth (Acts 16:13–15), who was a significant commercial merchant. Deborah was a judge (Judges 4–5). Jesus affirmed Mary when she chose to do traditional male activities, worship and study, rather than the traditional female work of preparing the meal (Luke 10:38–42). Paul writes that in Christ there is neither male nor female (Galatians 3:28).

Traditional assumptions about women's work patterns are changing in our culture. Unfortunately, though, some of the traditional assumptions are still used by some employers to justify limited job placement for women, lower pay scales, slow promotions, and other policies that restrict equity in employment. Christians should take the lead in finding ways to balance the tensions between family and work by striving to eliminate sex discrimination in the workplace, and at the same time finding creative ways for both men and women to share family responsibilities.

Discrimination Against the Disabled

People with disabilities are created in the image of God just as much as star athletes or homecoming queens. Yet psychological as well as physical barriers have been placed in their access to the workplace. They experience discrimination because of thoughtless assumptions that disabled people will be less productive or that they really don't want to work.

Such stereotypes are further reinforced by the fact that many people feel uncomfortable around people who are disabled. Because they have not taken the time to work through their own emotions, they don't know what to say to disabled people. Ignorance fosters feelings of insecurity, and the able-bodied end up revealing their own emotional handicaps.

Because there are certain costs associated with employing disabled persons, such as health insurance premiums or special equipment and facilities, some firms have not hired them. This has meant a loss both to business and to society. Disabled people have lost dignity and the sense of worth that comes from making a contribution to society. Society has lost the economic and social contribution disabled workers could have made.

Affirming the authenticity of the disabled does not mean that business must become a charity. It simply means that business should be equitable. People with disabilities should be allowed to work and earn what their productivity will justify. If business would take the minimal step of hiring the disabled and paying them their worth, the overwhelming majority of the disabled would not only prove their worth economically but find their self-respect greatly enhanced. What is not equitable is to deny them access to the marketplace and force them to remain nonproductive.

Age Discrimination

For many years Dick was employed as a book salesman for a Christian book publisher. He was very good at his job. He met and exceeded his quotas and got positive performance reviews. He was particularly good at selling Bibles.

Shortly after he turned fifty-five, however, his supervisor told Dick that he was sorry, but Dick was to be let go. Shortly afterward Dick learned that a younger person had been given his territory.

Dick tried to find out what had happened, but he couldn't get any information from the company. All he could conclude was that he was released because he cost too much. Because of his age and experience it cost the company more for his salary, health insurance, and other benefits than it would cost for a younger person. It looked to Dick as if he had been discriminated against because of his age.

Age discrimination is an increasing problem that hits older men and women at both ends of the job market: when they look for jobs (older workers generally have more experience and hence can ask a higher salary), and in situations like Dick's when they become eligible for benefits that are related to age. Both types of age discrimination are forbidden by law. But the problem persists because of the difficulty in proving that the real reason behind the failure to hire or the early release was age discrimination.

The Employee Retirement Income Security Act of 1974 (ERISA) was enacted largely because of mounting evidence that some employers were releasing older employees before a defined retirement date. ERISA mandated funding and provided vested interests in pension programs. Too many employers had been using economic downturns in their business as convenient opportunities to justify the release of senior employees before they became eligible for pensions.

Certainly an employer does have special obligations to a loyal employee who has given the most productive years of his or her life to the business. Age does bring with it a number of changes. Older employees are likely to file a disproportionate number of claims against their insurance coverage, because they tend to have more illnesses. They sometimes become less productive and less adaptable to change. On the other hand, they have valuable experience accumulated over many years. They are conscientious and loyal. Perhaps they could be assigned less physically demanding jobs. Or additional time could be taken to explain new procedures. Business should repay the faithfulness of long-term employees by being faithful to them.

The Right Employment Strategy

There are both moral and economic reasons for eliminating discrimination. The moral reasons are based on the fact that since all people are created in the image of God, they are responsible to do productive work. It is wrong to use discriminatory practices to deny individuals and groups of people the opportunity to work. The economic reasons are illustrated in the following story.

When you are handling $36,000 worth of hotel reservations every hour, it's important to have reliable staff on hand. You can't afford no-show employees. So when a winter storm paralyzed Atlanta last year, the Days Inns national reservation center followed its policy of transporting employees to and from the job. Interestingly it was only the "young and able-bodied" who needed help. The senior and wheelchair-bound workers all came in on their own steam.

That typifies the lodging chain's experience with "special sector employees" (mostly seniors and handicapped, with some homeless). The company began seriously recruiting this untapped sector of the work force four years ago and has found them to be more dependable and motivated than employees between eighteen and thirty-five. On weekends, for example, the no-show rate among the younger set can be as high as 40 percent; among seniors and disabled workers it's zero. "Their enthusiasm serves as a role model for the balance of the employees," says the company's vice-president of human relations.[2]

Christians should take the lead in developing policies and procedures that eliminate current discriminatory practices and that attempt to make up for past discrimination. Many Christians are doing just that. The U.S. Bishops' "Pastoral Letter on Catholic Social Teaching and the U.S. Economy," and the Lay Commission on Catholic Social Teaching's book, *Toward the Future: Catholic Social Thought and the U.S. Economy*, both address many of these issues with a deep concern for social justice for the less advantaged.

If we are to make progress in eliminating discrimination we must go beyond generalized good intentions to specific commitments, policies, and practices for affirmative action. The following list suggests some specific ideas that should be included in a plan.

1. A written commitment and goals for affirmative action and equal employment approved by the board of directors and top management.
2. The designation of a specific person with responsibility to implement the plan.
3. Constant monitoring of the plan for evaluating and measuring effectiveness and the designation of a specific person to carry this responsibility.
4. A profile of the numbers of women, racial minorities, and disabled in various employment categories and departments.
5. A description of procedures that are to be used in recruitment, employment, and promotion to assure fairness to all groups.

If we follow these steps, we will open doors to all who want to work. Skills will be available that otherwise would have been excluded. The greater diversity in the work force will enrich the workplace. Many strategies are available to accomplish this. One business owner might design a shift schedule to accommodate mothers who desire to see their children off to school. Another might hire minority employees via contacts in a local black church. Still others might redesign work stations for the elderly and wheelchair bound. The creative possibilities are endless.

QUESTIONS FOR REFLECTION

Work Is a Healing Process

1. What may have happened to the man in this story if he had never had the opportunity to work?
2. Whose responsibility is it to find work for those who are hard to employ? The people themselves? Private employers? Government?

Exploring the Bible

1. Read Proverbs 31:10–31. How does this passage describe the role of a married woman?
2. Read Luke 14:12–14. Are employment opportunities part of the banquet to which we should invite the disadvantaged? When and by whom will Christians who respond to this call be rewarded?
3. Read Ephesians 2:11–22. What can we learn from this conflict between the Jews and Gentiles about discrimination in the workplace?

Contemporary Comment

1. Tony Campolo writes the following:

Political demonstrations don't lift people out of the cycle of poverty. Only jobs lift people out of the cycle of poverty. Christians have been slow catching on to this. We go to the poor in our cities and say, "We're here to serve you. What can we do?" And they yell, "Give us jobs." So we set up a legal clinic and a basketball league. Next year we come back and ask, "What do you need?" And they yell really loud, "We need jobs!" So we set up a pregnancy crisis center and a food co-op. Eventually they stop asking for jobs, because they understand that we're not really asking, "What do you need?" but "What do you need that we know how to do?"[3]

What can Christians do to make jobs available to people of inner city North America?

2. Imagine you are the supervisor of a shop in which all the workers are of a particular ethnic group which historically has been antagonistic to outsiders. Of two equally qualified applicants, should you choose the one who will (in your opinion) cause the least disruption (stress) within the existing group?

3. Explore the reasons women work in the paid labor force. Is it because of economic need? Extras for the family? Self-fulfillment? Social contact? Should employers actively seek out or discourage more women employees at all levels of the organization?

4. Consider whether Christians should hire only other Christians to work in their companies.

5. If we want older people to remain productive, what implications does that have for retraining programs?

NOTES

1. From Max DePree, "The Process of Work: Is This a Brother Keeping Business?" *The Reformed Journal* (May 1979): 10. Copyright Wm. B. Eerdmans Publishing Co. Used by permission.
2. Bill Stack, "Jobs Available: Homeless and Seniors Encouraged to Apply," *Management Review* (August 1989): 13–16.
3. Quotation from Tony Campolo in "Your Career Can Make a Difference?" Promotional brochure for Evangelical Association for the Promotion of Education (January 1987).

Chapter 8

HUMAN DEVELOPMENT IN THE WORKPLACE

POINT FOR DISCUSSION

Curse or Blessing

Mike Lefevre, Steelworker

You can't take pride anymore. You remember when a guy could point to a house he built, how many logs he stacked. He built it and he was proud of it.

It's hard to take pride in a bridge you're never gonna cross, in a door you're never gonna open. You're mass-producing things and you never see the end result of it. I worked for a trucker one time. And I got this tiny satisfaction when I loaded a truck. At least I could see the truck depart loaded. In a steel mill, forget it. You don't see where nothing goes.

I got chewed out by my foreman once. He said, "Mike, you're a good worker but you have a bad attitude." My attitude is that I don't get excited about my job. I do my work but I don't say whoopee-doo. The day I get excited about my job is the day I go to a head shrinker. How are you gonna get excited about pullin' steel? How are you gonna get excited when you're tired and want to sit down?

It's not just the work. Somebody built the pyramids. Somebody's going to build something. Pyramids, Empire

State Building—these things just don't happen. There's hard work behind it. I would like to see a building, say, the Empire State, I would like to see on one side of it a foot-wide strip from top to bottom with the name of every bricklayer, the name of every electrician, with all the names. So when a guy walked by, he could take his son and say, "See, that's me over there on the forty-fifth floor. I put the steel beam in." Picasso can point to a painting. What can I point to? A writer can point to a book. Everybody should have something to point to.

Carl Murray Bates, Stonemason

Every piece of stone you pick up is different, the grain's a little different and this and that. It'll split one way and break the other. You pick up your stone and look at it and make an educated guess. It's a pretty good day layin' stone or brick. Not tiring. Anything you like to do isn't tiresome. It's hard work; stone is heavy. At the same time, you get interested in what you're doing and you usually fight the clock the other way. You're not lookin' for quittin.' You're wondering why you haven't got enough done and it's almost quittin' time.

There's not a house in this country that I haven't built that I don't look at every time I go by. (Laughs) I can sit here now and actually in my mind see so many that you wouldn't believe. If there's one stone in there crooked, I know where it's at and I'll never forget it. Maybe thirty years, I'll know a place where I should have took that stone out and redone it but I didn't. I still notice it. The people who live there might not notice it, but I notice it. I never pass that house that I don't think of it. I've got one house in mind right now. (Laughs) That's the work of my hands. 'Cause you see, stone, you don't repaint it, you don't camouflage it. It's there, just like I left it forty years ago.

I can't imagine a job where you go home and maybe go by a year later and you don't know what you've done. My work,

> I can see what I did the first day I started. All my work is set right out there in the open and I can look at it as I go by. It's something I can see the rest of my life.[1]

Stewards of Human Creativity

Mike Lefevre and Carl Bates have different attitudes toward their work. At first glance it might seem that the problem is Mike's attitude. But look a bit deeper.

Paul Goodman, a sociologist, wrote a number of years ago about what he called "meaningful work." He suggested that there has been a subtle change in the nature of work that robs it of its meaning. To be meaningful, he said, work needs to have an element of creativity. Workers must be able to see part of themselves in the finished product. They must be able to say, "I made it. I see my personal touch in the final product. When I see the product I feel a sense of pride because I made it."

Much work in our world today does not allow that sense of pride. It is not easy for the assembly line worker who hour after hour, day after day, punches out a small valve hidden in the middle of an automobile engine to see his craftsmanship in the finished car. If bosses do not allow the people they work with to participate in meaningful decisions they won't be able to feel ownership and creativity in their work.

Mike's problem was far deeper than one of attitude. He was doing meaningless work. His attitude resulted from the way his work was organized. The organization for which he worked structured his job so that he could not see part of himself in the finished product.

We are God's agents of human development in the workplace. If we serve in management positions we have a special responsibility to organize work so that it is meaningful and creative rather than demeaning.

Talents are given by God, and developed by people. God told Moses about Bezalel: "I have filled him with the spirit of God, with skill, ability, and knowledge in all kinds of crafts—to make artistic designs for work in gold, silver, bronze, to cut and set stones, to work in wood and to engage in all kinds of craftsmanship" (Exodus 31:3–5). Although we are given great discretion in the use of our talents, our abilities were not simply given to us as individuals for our personal enjoyment and identity. They are intended for the benefit of others.

Bezalel was to use his skills to build the Tent of Meeting and the Ark of the Testimony, to be used by all the people in worship. As spiritual gifts are given to individuals in the church to serve the entire body, so individuals are given talents to benefit those with whom they work and the whole human community.

The parable of the talents clearly describes our responsibility for the talents God provides. A master, going on a trip, gave three stewards money to use until he returned. Two stewards were productive with it and were rewarded. The third buried his money and wasted the opportunity to earn interest on it. He was cast out of the kingdom (Matthew 25:14–30). Business organizations should not be equated with God's kingdom, but the parable's truth is transferable. God is keenly interested in our talents and ideas and does not want them to lie dormant and be wasted.

Developing ourselves and others is not an end in itself. It is part of our worship of God to develop and use the skills God has given. Our own renewal in the image of God is enhanced as we seek the full development of ourselves and those with whom we work.

As Christians in business we have many opportunities to encourage the development of existing talents and to help discover latent talents. Business already recognizes the benefit of this. Industry spends billions of dollars every year on training and development programs. In many cases it is cheaper to develop the raw material on hand—the underdeveloped employee—than to purchase the "finished goods"—the polished employee—in the open market.

Theories of Management

Business has spent a lot of time during the last quarter of a century developing theories of management that help us understand how to manage most effectively. All of these theories were built on particular assumptions about human behavior and motives. We will look at only one of these. Christian managers need to examine thoughtfully the assumptions and theories that guide their actions.

Three contrasting management-style typologies are Theory X, Theory Y, and Theory Z. Each of these describes a kind of employee matched with a particular management style. Each also suggests that one style is "better." Douglas McGregor presented Theories X and Y in his classic *The Human Side of Enterprise*. William Ouchi described Theory Z in a recent book by that title.

McGregor's interest lay in the full development of human potential, as he understood it. These so-called theories are really polarities of a continuum of management styles. Theory X represents management by direction and control, and assumes that workers by nature tend to be noncreative, unambitious, security-oriented people who respond to a stick more readily than a carrot. This style of management assumes that employees see work only as a necessary evil and avoid it if possible. The key to management under Theory X is strong discipline, strict rules, and constant control. Mike Lefevre seems to reflect the approach of a Theory X employee.

According to Theory Y, on the other hand, work is as natural as play. It assumes that people want to express creativity, exercise self-control, and seek responsibility through their work. Therefore they want to participate in setting objectives and making decisions. The key to good management is providing persons with interesting work and appropriate rewards. The carrot is seen as being more effective than the stick. Carl Bates is a model Theory Y employee. Theory Y was widely acclaimed as capable of meeting emerging employee needs as society moved from a predominantly manufacturing econ-omy to a service economy, where social and educational skills played a larger role.

Professor Ouchi offered a third management model, Theory Z, based on his examination of Japanese management styles. This theory emphasizes human interdependence, trust, and company loyalty. Internal company competition is softened with greater teamwork and a spirit of cooperation. It encourages a broader social consciousness, and the subtleties of business manners come to the fore.

Which of these theories of management is most compatible with Christian principles? If we view work as a necessary evil and employees as people to be directed and controlled, we would likely use Theory X. On the other hand, if we see work as a fulfilling part of life and employees as persons wanting to grow and develop in their work, we would use Theory Y or Z.

Christian managers should reject much of Theory X because of its lopsided view of human nature. It emphasizes only the worst traits of repressed and unloved people. Theory X tends to create employees who are dependent and who do not develop decision-making and creative skills. Only a small minority of businesses today operate primarily on the negative traits of Theory X.

Unfortunately Theory Y, while appealing to the expansive and laudable capacities of human nature, ignores the reality that many people have chosen to be selfish and self-centered. Some do not want to work and need the threat of punishment to get anything done. All of us have a bit of that spirit in us.

Theory Z attempts to build levels of trust and mutual respect, but it tends to ignore the real differences in interest between employees and employers. It also does not give enough attention to human alienation and self-centeredness. It can be manipulative.

Imagine that you are the teacher in a class of beginning business students. How you manage the class is fundamentally a manage-ment decision. Will you use Theory X, Y, or Z?

The first thing you need to discover is the characteristics of your students. You need to examine your own assumptions about people in general and about students specifically. You also want to do some empirical research. You might ask students why they are in the class. Is it a required class that they really do not want to attend, or is it an elective class that they take because they want to be there? What level of skill do they bring to the class? Are they basically lazy, or do they want to learn? If they are lazy and don't want to be there, you may need to use Theory X. Otherwise you may want to use Y or Z.

You also need to ask what kind of students you want to have when they finish the class. Do you want them to be dependent and able to follow orders well without thinking? If so you will probably use Theory X. Or do you want them to develop skills of independent thinking and trust in collaborative decision making? If you want this kind of student to emerge from your class you would likely use Theory Y or Z.

This little example shows a number of things. First of all it shows both the strengths and limitations of these theories. There are many things these theories do not consider, yet they do provide a framework in which to look at certain questions. Not all people will respond as the theories suggest they might.

This example also shows that each of these theories and all other theories that are used to influence human behavior contain implicit value assumptions. For example, the question about the kind of students you want to have leave your class is a value question.

Each of these theories is in touch with certain aspects of human nature, but none by itself adequately captures the complexity of human behavior. The value question must be answered from the perspective of faith. There is no "Christian" theory of management. But there are principles, which when integrated with other theories, do suggest how Christians should carry out their management responsibilities.

God expects us to have dominion over land resources, buildings, airline schedules, water pollution, and many other things.

But our management of other people should be different and unique. The Scriptures talk a lot about servanthood. It is not natural to approach management theory from the perspective of servanthood, yet that is exactly what we are called to do. It is a very different approach from the power-based views of many secular managers. A further exploration of Christian love and its commitment to service will help us add a Christian perspective to contemporary management theories.

Love: A Style of Management

"Management" carries much symbolic meaning. Typical definitions suggest that managers use all resources, including people, by directing and controlling them to accomplish an organizational objective. A manager is a person with an assigned responsibility who has been given the authority and power to accomplish an assigned task and who is accountable for getting it done. Many older definitions of management emphasize concepts like control, direct, command, and boss. These imply a top-down approach. But, both from within industry and from Christians in management, a new concept is emerging. Among Christians this is sometimes called "servant leadership."

The word "servant" is a biblical concept that conveys the idea of working for and at the direction of someone else. It is enabling rather than directive. Christ's response to the mother of James and John, who asked that her sons be allowed to sit on his left and right hand in his kingdom, is instructive:

You know that the rulers of the Gentiles lord it over them, and their high officials exercise authority over them. Not so with you. Instead, whoever wants to become great among you must be your servant, and whosoever wants to be first must be your slave; just as the Son of Man did not come to be served, but to serve, and to give his life as a ransom for many. (Matthew 20:25–28)

The implication is that we too must follow Christ's example and be servants to others around us.

Some Christians will argue that Christ was simply making a distinction in this passage between action of the world (Gentiles lording it over their subjects) and actions as servants in the church. These people believe that Christ would not have told his disciples to serve the ten workers employed in their fishing business. They might reason that business is in the business of providing goods and services and not in the business of developing human potential. From their perspective human development is best left to the family and church. Therefore they would suggest Christian managers serve those under them best when everyone knows who is the boss. They suggest that since managers have power to get things done they should use it forcefully. There is another perspective. Christian managers will try to model the love of Christ in their work.

In Ephesians Paul dealt with such superior subordinate relationships when he told the Christian slaves to obey their masters, not with lip service, but from the heart, as to Christ. He told them this was the will of God and that they were to render their service, "as to the Lord, and not to men." Yet, when Paul addressed Christian masters, he said, "...do the same things to them [slaves], and give up threatening, knowing that both their Master and yours is in heaven, and there is no partiality with Him" (Ephesians 6:9 NASB). Clearly Paul wanted both masters as well as slaves to first recognize their servanthood to God.

How, then, is a manager to act? The appropriate strategy is not one of manipulation. The slaves were told not to just render service that looked good—"with eye-service"—but to work from the heart for Christ as they served their masters. It is not acceptable for a manager to be deceitfully manipulative to get results.

The best strategy is one that uses power carefully. Christ had power. He was a very persuasive person and could move people to act. His real power was expressed in his love. He could have called down an army of angels to do his will, but he did not. That was not his approach, even though he had such power. Instead he used love.

His love today is not some mushy emotion, sentimental work, or superficial action. It is careful, conscious action that does what is right and necessary for the building up of his children. Love comforts us on one occasion and strictly disciplines us on another. It teaches us at one moment and lets us look and search for answers for long periods of time on other occasions.

Managers have power, too. It is part of their position. Yet they do not have to flaunt it. Instead our power as managers can be contained in love. Love is what is needed to enhance, build up, mature, and strengthen the cared-for person. Love is the most powerful force in the world. It is a force of spirit, not muscle.

Love: A Way to Work with People

If Christians cannot love those with whom they work, they cannot be capable managers from a Christian perspective. They may be stimulators, manipulators, operators, motivators, or demanders; but not managers. In a biblical sense, managers must love those with whom they work. Yet loving someone after the fifth mistake is hard work. Loving the person who fails to meet an important deadline is taxing. Loving the unmotivated is tiring. Loving the complainer is trying. But agape love is not an emotional love. It is an action word embodying a commitment of the "will" to do what is right from God's perspective. Love is a right response to a need. It will involve the fruits of the Spirit, patience, kindness, gentleness, faithfulness, goodness, and self-control.

Think for a minute about Jack. He is slow adjusting to the new edition of Lotus 1-2-3™ for his computer. We could make him feel incompetent and undermine his identity in a time of stress; or we could remind him of his past demonstrated competency and assure him that it will return soon enough as he moves up the learning curve. To love means to recognize Jack's need to feel accepted and to feel competent.

Loving our coworkers, our peers, and our superiors means focusing on their long-term best interest. We are to look out for the interests of others and not merely our own (Philippians 2:4). Love is not a role to assume; love is an inner attitude, a conscious mental commitment that translates into actions benefiting others. It is reflected in the Christian's obligation to care for the whole person.

It means we consider our subordinates' long-term interests when we manage. Suppose you, a production manager, are consulted about required production time for a large, one-time, special order of fabricated countertops. Pressure is inherent in this request. Your superiors ask, "How soon can you have them ready?" Corporate profitability is at stake. You have commitments to other long-standing customers and their previously placed orders. You worry about how you as a manager are perceived by your superiors. But along with these considerations should come concern for the quality of life of the fabrication workers who will make the countertops. The pressures associated with production ultimately fall on them. They must work more rapidly. They must put in the overtime hours. Make no mistake about it, a decision like this will affect the workers' families, too. The pressure of this special order will go home. If the pressures are too great and for too long, love may require a recommendation to bypass this opportunity. It may not be in employees' best interests.

Love: A Costly Choice

The manager and owner of several supermarkets in a small town in eastern Pennsylvania became aware that a checkout clerk was stealing money. His first impulse and that of the others in the business who had been aware of the problem for some time was to fire the employee. But the owner took another approach.

The owner confronted the dishonest clerk with the clear message that the stealing could not continue. He also arranged counseling to help the clerk work through financial problems she was having at home and arranged closer supervision to make the temptation less. All of that took time and money. If this story were fiction it would end by saying that the clerk became a hard-working, honest employee and paid all the money back. That didn't happen. After some months she stole again. And then after several more months, again.

The owner continued to have patience over several years. He lost the money that was stolen. He invested a lot in providing extra supervision and in providing counseling. There was a lot of dissatisfaction among the other employees, who thought he was too soft. Yet, through the entire experience, he tried to act in ways that he thought were best for the employee and that demonstrated God's forgiving love.

This is not the only approach that demonstrates love. Sometimes tough love is best. The director of a church-sponsored school in an overseas setting faced a similar problem. A trusted employee forged signatures and cashed four checks. The total amounted to about three times the employee's annual salary. The director needed to decide whether or not to involve the police. He knew that the evidence was strong and that the employee would likely spend many years in prison.

The director, after much consultation with other Christians, decided to report to the police and at the same time arrange with the court to suspend a prison sentence while the employee paid back the money by continuing work at the school. Since the amount was so large, he suggested forgiving a sizable part. The employee would be arrested and spend several weeks in jail awaiting trial. That, plus the repayment, seemed like a good way to help the employee face the consequences of a wrong act and at the same time rebuild his life. This story does not have a fictional ending either. During the trial the judge ignored the agreement and sentenced the employee to nine months in jail.

The director visited the employee during the term and helped him attend college after release. The employee said many times that the whole experience was good and helped him turn his life in a different direction.

One of the biggest temptations we all face in business is to become so absorbed with our products and services that we treat people as mere factors of production and means to an end. This is almost natural because people, like other resources, are employed in many impersonal functions that produce economic wealth. People can be seen only as costs. We can be tempted to treat them only as a means to success.

Decision making becomes far more complex when we take people seriously. When every person and every individual act has a larger value than just the bottom line, decisions become more difficult.

Imagine that you are the supervisor of a plant that receives a large special rush order. It would be easy to turn up the pressure, apply more force, and get the order out. Pharaoh tried that when he ordered his slave drivers to make the Israelites gather their own straw to make bricks, and at the same time to force them to make the same number of bricks as before (Exodus 5:7–18).

If we take people seriously, however, we will take a different approach. We will need to consult with assembly workers to see if they can handle the special order. We may need to ask regular customers if we can delay the delivery of their orders. We might even check for excess plant capacity in a nearby competitor that we could lease for the short term. These actions take time and creativity. They greatly complicate the decision process.

Concern for others might cost us promotions and hurt our own careers in some firms where the corporate culture is not sensitive to people. Some managers would interpret actions like that of the supermarket manager as a sign of poor management and lack of courage to make hard decisions. Normally, however, genuine love is welcomed and is well received in most companies. It's hard to imagine that Bethlehem Steel or Inland Steel would be totally unconcerned about someone like Mike Lefevre.

It takes time and money to care for people. It takes time to listen. It takes time to think about them and respond appropriately. It takes time and money and creativity to implement programs and procedures that take people's needs into consideration. It takes time to find and develop people's abilities and talents. Love is hard work and it is costly.

Love: Practical Wisdom

One of the more intriguing issues faced by business professionals is the appropriate use of organizational politics. We can use organizational politics to protect ourselves and our self-interest, or as a resource to implement love in the workplace. Does that sound strange? Our use of the term "politics" may be a bit misleading. When people play politics for selfish and manipulative reasons they are wrong. What we mean here is a thoughtful sensitivity to finding the least obtrusive way of getting things done. Organizational politics can be the oil that smooths organizational relationships.

One can argue that even Pharaoh should have been more politically astute. His harsh action ultimately led not to the production of more bricks, but to the loss of his whole labor force. The Bible tells Christians to be "wise as serpents and harmless as doves" (Matthew 10:16).

Luke 16 includes a fascinating story of a manager who did not manage well. The manager sensed that his master was displeased and that he would soon be fired. So he went to his master's creditors and reduced their debts. He wanted to have friends after he lost his job. The master commended the manager not for his dishonesty, but for his cleverness. Jesus used this story to suggest that Christians should be just as creative and clever in working in the world for kingdom values as this manager was in taking care of his own needs.

In its worst sense office politics is manipulative, self-serving, unscrupulous behavior that incorporates compromise and the dilution of ethical values. In its best sense being political means that we are practically wise, prudent, diplomatic, courteous, and honor those to whom honor is due (1 Peter 2:17). As Christian businesspeople we should remember the warnings of Proverbs to help use political strategy carefully:

The man of integrity walks securely, but he who takes crooked paths will be found out. (Proverbs 10:9)

The tongue of the wise makes knowledge acceptable, but the mouth of fools spouts folly. (Proverbs 15:2 NASB)

Plans fail for lack of counsel, but with many advisors they succeed. (Proverbs 15:22)

Paul gives us similar advice in recounting his trip to Jerusalem to explain his ministry to the Gentiles. He first "did this privately to those who seemed to be leaders" before he spoke before the entire group (Galatians 2:2). Why? Because it would have been impolite and unwise to surprise the other leaders, in public, with charges they had not had time to contemplate privately.

Showing respect, being courteous, and giving honor is not licking boots or buttering-up people. It is not compromise to express your convictions politely and quietly, at appropriate times, and in ways that do not embarrass others.

Scott, a college student, worked one summer for a roofing company. One day he was assigned to put a roof on the new plant being built in his community to manufacture a popular beer. Scott believes that his commitment to Jesus Christ requires him to not use alcoholic beverages because of the death and violence they cause. He could not conscientiously work at the beer-manufacturing facility.

Scott decided that since he had made a commitment to the roofing company it was not fair for him to refuse to work at the last minute. So he very respectfully told his supervisor of his conviction and said that he could not work at the plant in the future even if it meant that he would need to resign. But he agreed to work that one day so that the agency would have time to find a replacement.

His boss expressed appreciation for his convictions and assigned him to other jobs.

Another area where political sensitivity is important is in encouraging firms to adopt policies that reflect Christian principles. For example, we might want to suggest that a firm make contributions to a local charity. We could give all kinds of arguments from a Christian perspective why such a gift should be given. However, if we work for a publicly owned firm, we might want to promote our concerns by arguing that they are practical and in the long-term best interest of the company. It is not compromise to use pragmatic arguments.

The theme of this chapter has been human development in the workplace. There is no greater opportunity and challenge for Christians in business than to find innovative ways to make work meaningful and to create workplace environments which stimulate employees to develop new skills and to grow to become more whole persons. The key that unlocks this approach is love: love that controls our attitudes and actions and makes us into servant leaders.

QUESTIONS FOR REFLECTION

Work: Curse or Blessing

1. Compare the comments about the nature of work given by the two workers in the Point for Discussion. Why does one enjoy his work while the other hates his job?
2. If these workers were Christian, should they both love their work? Should Christians despise any kind of work?

Exploring the Bible

1. Read Genesis 1:28; 2:15; and 3:17–19. When God created humans, what was the nature of work? How did work change after Adam and Eve disobeyed God?
2. Read 2 Thessalonians 3:6–13. Why are the Thessalonians urged to work? Is Paul too harsh on those who do not work?
3. Read 1 Corinthians 13:1–13. How should the concepts of Christian love found in this passage affect our relationships at work?

Contemporary Comment

1. React to the quote below:

Work is my primary expression of faith and praise to God, my service to the neighbors He commands me to love, my responsible stewardship of his gifts, and the most effective means of communicating the good news of salvation to the world.[2]

Will paid employment fulfill all our work responsibilities before God? Do you agree that work is the most effective way to share the gospel? Would Christian love in the workplace ever require that we restrain open Christian witnessing on the job?

2. Think about an assignment or job where you failed. Why did you fail? Was it your fault? How did you feel?

3. Would you rather work in a company whose style was shaped by Theory X, Theory Y, or Theory Z? Is any of them more compatible than the others with Christian views on people at work?

4. Suppose you see Sarah, a check-out clerk you supervise, put $20 from the register in her pocket just before closing. She's been with the company a year without any problems. Company policy states that employee theft will result in termination. Sarah's a single mother of two. What does love require?

NOTES

1. From Studs Terkel, *Working: People Talk About What They Do All Day and How They Feel About What They Do* (New York: Random House, 1972), xxi–xxii and xlvi–xlix. Copyright © 1972, 1974 by Studs Terkel. Reprinted by permission of Pantheon Books, a Division of Random House, Inc.

2. From Judith Shelley, *Not Just a Job* (Downer's Grove, IL: InterVarsity Press, 1985), 30.

Chapter 9

THE JUNGLE OF OBLIGATIONS AND RIGHTS

POINT FOR DISCUSSION

Workers Strike Over Drug Testing Proposal

"INDIANAPOLIS—Workers at Kerr-McGee Chemical Corporation's Forest Products Division went on strike Thursday over a management proposal to begin mandatory, random drug testing.

The thirty-three hourly workers at the plant, which manufactures railroad ties, struck after their union contract expired at midnight Wednesday.

Louis D. Ridley, a spokesman for the Oil, Chemical, and Atomic Workers International Union, said the proposed drug-testing policy is the only strike issue. No new contract talks were scheduled, he said. The company wants the new contract with the union's Local 7706 to include a policy requiring employees to submit to random drug tests. Under the proposed policy, any worker who tested positive for drug use, or refused to take the test, would be fired.

Plant superintendent Mike Evancho said management believes the strict policy is necessary for safety, though he knew of no accidents in the past that could be traced to drug use.

'We want to provide a safe working environment for our employees, and the way to do this is to have a drug-free environment,' Evancho said.

Union representatives maintain, however, that the policy would constitute an invasion of the worker's privacy.

'We're concerned about safety, but there is no particular drug problem at the plant,' said William Scanlon, president of the local. Evancho said the proposed policy would include a 30-day grace period during which employees with drug abuse problems could come forward, receive treatment, and not be penalized.

'That's a good idea,' said Richard A. Waples, an attorney for the Indiana Civil Liberties Union. 'But not just for a month. That should be standard operation procedure.' "

Waples said he believes that proposed policy would violate the workers' civil rights, and said similar policies have been successfully challenged in court.[1]

Defining Obligations and Rights

The concept of rights is deeply rooted in North American society. Think how often you have said, "I have a right to . . . " The Declaration of Independence talks of "inalienable rights . . . endowed by the creator." The first ten amendments to the Constitution are called the "Bill of Rights." There are student rights, minority rights, rights of women and men, rights of children, and rights of the elderly. The Point for Discussion identifies a very practical situation in which there is a conflict between the rights of employees to privacy and the rights of a business to have a drug-free environment.

The concept of rights provides a very useful framework for thinking about the responsibilities of managers and firms to employees. Although some people dismiss appeals to rights as merely an inappropriate way to take care of oneself, concerns about rights in the workplace are appropriate. Instead of ignoring them we should start with a clearer understanding of rights and obligations. Then we should put that understanding within a biblical framework and apply it to practical business issues we confront daily.

People disagree on a precise definition of rights. John Locke referred to a right as something that, by definition, is possessed unconditionally by everyone. This is what is meant by the Declaration of Independence when it lists "inalienable rights." Rights have also been defined as legitimate moral claims, the enjoyment of which society ought to guarantee in writing. The right to be protected from discrimination based on race or sex is one example. Other such claims are specified and protected by law, such as the right to vote, to own property, and to receive a publicly funded education. There are other unwritten but implied moral rights, such as the right of every person to be treated with respect and to be told the truth.

John Warwick Montgomery, in his book *Human Rights and Human Dignity*, points to three types of rights in the economic and political arena. First are basic human rights, or civil liberties, associated with protection from political authority. An example is the Bill of Rights, which protects individuals against undue encroachment by political authorities into private affairs. A second type of right guarantees the availability of certain benefits provided by government, such as the right to an education, the right to social security, and the right to observe certain national holidays. The third type of right applies to sharing the world's resources, and includes the right to a clean environment and to economic, social, and political development.

Rights function in several ways in society. First, they provide guidelines that regulate the relationships between individuals and institutions. Rights suggest what individuals and organizations can legitimately expect from each other. The Apostle Paul exerted his right as a Roman citizen to escape a flogging in Acts 22:22–29. He expected to be protected by the government. Employers have a right to expect productive work from employees. Employees have a right to expect a fair wage in return. Because free speech is considered to be a right in North America, people expect to be allowed to say what they think. Where free speech is not considered to be a right, people need to be much more careful about what they say. The fact that one person cannot borrow another's car without asking permission is an example of the right of private property ownership. Private property ownership regulates our relationships and expectations in regard to material goods.

Second, rights identify broadly shared assumptions about what things should be provided by a society. In our society everyone has a right to twelve years of government-provided education. Programs and strategies are developed to make sure that no one is excluded from this opportunity. Public funding is provided. We are less consistent in our approach to consumer rights, minority shareholder rights, and employment rights. There are a lot of disagreements about what things should be provided by society and what things should be provided by each individual and family for themselves.

In the past few years the whole issue of the right of housing has come to the attention of the American public as the number of homeless people keeps growing. Should everyone have a right to a decent house, just as they have a right to an education?

The third function of rights is to set limits. The right to privacy limits the kinds of questions a job interviewer can ask a prospective employee. Only personal information that is directly related to job performance can be requested. Most colleges will not share private phone numbers of students to protect their privacy. The right to privacy also limits the kinds of information a business can share from a confidential file.

People disagree on which desires are rights and which are merely preferences. Calling something a right gives it special status, because societies develop mechanisms to guarantee that rights are honored. Yet many desirable things should not be considered rights. For example, although nearly everyone would agree that it is desirable to have a driver's license, most states make the point that having a driver's license is a privilege, not a right. The privilege of having a driver's license must be earned by passing a test and demonstrating skill. It is not always clear which desirable things should be considered rights.

Assumptions about rights shift with changes in culture and values. In the United States black men did not have the right to vote until after the Civil War. Women did not have that right until 1920. In some countries elementary education is not considered a right as it is in North America. Access to health care is considered a right in Canada, but not in the United States. Some countries, like the Soviet Union, protect the right of everyone to have a job.

The issue of rights is particularly important for Christians in business. We need to protect the rights of others as we conduct business. We also need to contribute our understandings to the constantly changing debate in society about rights of employers and employees.

Rights always imply obligations. These are two sides of the same coin. A right is a legitimate claim one party can make on another party. That claim then places an obligation on the second party. For example, an employee's right to privacy places an obligation on an employer to protect confidential records. An employer's right to expect quality work places an obligation on employees to give their best. As Christians we should take both sides seriously as we sort out our understanding of this issue. Both parties, employers and employees, have rights as well as obligations.

The Sources of Obligations and Rights

Christians start with a unique understanding of the source of obligations and rights. Paul Marshall writes in *The Banner* that "the root of all human rights and authority is the righteousness and justice of God manifested in Jesus."[2] It is God's will that we practice justice. We are also created in the image of God. These facts give us legitimate claims to social, political, and economic arrangements that support justice and empower people. Often such claims are embodied in the concept of rights: the right to work, the right to be informed about decisions that affect us, the right to a safe work environment, and a host of other employee rights.

It is because God cares for us and protects us that we have these rights. God upholds justice by defending the rights of those who suffer injustice. He calls us to join in that task with special concern for the afflicted, the needy, the poor, and the powerless, whose rights are so often overlooked (Proverbs 29:7; 31: 8–9). Some laws give unfair advantage to segments of society or impose unjust burdens, such as Pharaoh did to the Israelites. The Old Testament prophets spoke loudly against such injustice. Amos wrote eloquently of our responsibility for the disadvantaged. In similar cases in contemporary business, it is legitimate to speak up for the rights of others.

Sometimes societies and organizations develop agreements on rights and obligations that are not necessarily compatible with God's will. For example, many Christians feel that abortion for the sake of convenience is wrong, even though it is legal in many states. Some Christians feel killing in self-defense or in war is against Jesus' teaching to love our enemies, even though killing in these circumstances is considered a right in most countries. Similarly, in business, our legal right to strategies that undercut competitors may not always square with our Christian values. We must be careful to distinguish rights that emanate from God's justice from legal rights in society. To be godly often requires going far beyond merely being legal.

For Christians a discussion of rights in business must always relate to God's justice and God's concern for people. Our task is to discern the mind of Christ so that we will fill those obligations and defend those rights that reflect God's will. The difficult part for many of us is determining God's will in specific situations.

Most of us in business would agree that we have a special responsibility to honor and protect the rights of others. It is less clear when and under what circumstances we should stick up for our own rights.

Asserting and claiming rights can sometimes result from pride or selfishness. Strident demands for recognition of rights can contradict the biblical call to servanthood and humility. The Bible asks us to serve others and to seek the rights of others. It says we should accept suffering and wrong rather than retaliate or take revenge. Jesus stood meekly before his accusers and accepted their verdict of crucifixion. In that situation he did not defend his rights, though he had the power to do so.

Therefore, when we face situations where rights are not honored, whether the injustice is done to us or to another person or group, we must thoughtfully choose our response. Injustice in business is always wrong, but there are a number of ways to confront it.

Sometimes we should voluntarily give up even legitimate rights. We should endure inconvenience or even suffering or financial loss in order to serve. This is what the Bible means when it talks about taking up the cross of Jesus (Matthew 10:37–39; Luke 9:23–25). Several years ago Earl, a Christian businessperson, loaned a distant relative money to buy a house. The relative ran onto hard times and was unable to repay the loan or the interest. Earl had a strong case and a right to sue to collect the debt. If he had won, the house would have been sold to pay the loan. Earl chose not to sue. He took a big loss because he did not want to cause additional hurt.

We should not always be quiet. Sometimes justice requires that we state our rights and defend them vigorously. We sometimes allow injustice to continue because we are afraid to confront it. Mary Ellen is a Christian. Several years ago she worked in a southern Florida office in which her boss verbally abused everyone. Her coworkers were afraid that if they complained they would be fired; but Mary Ellen determined that it was her responsibility to stand up for her right to be treated fairly and decently. She confronted her boss in a firm but kind way, saying that she and the other office personnel had a right to be treated with respect. She threatened to report the abuse to the president of the company. Her willingness to claim her rights, even at some risk to her job, opened conversation that led to change and improved working conditions in the entire office.

In some situations our sense of rights differs from society's, and we must make costly choices. In California a Christian landlord who refused to rent an apartment to an unmarried couple was sued. Earlier court cases had determined that couples have a right to rent the apartment no matter what their marital status. Thus the law required the landlord to rent the apartment to them—even though she felt it was morally wrong to do so. In this case and others Christians conscientiously oppose granting something society has determined to be a right.

There are times when we must pay a high cost for standing up for rights that society does not honor. Rosa Parks began the civil rights movement by asserting her right to sit at the front of a bus. Many people in this country and elsewhere have served prison terms because they had the courage to stand up for their rights.

We must sometimes be willing to pay a price for standing up for rights and for fulfilling obligations. It may be the cost of resistance for being out of step with the general public. In business there are times when we will need to pay the cost of being responsive to employees and determining our Christian obligations toward them. The topics that follow are four examples of issues in which the issues of rights and obligations are crucial.

Family Rights in the Workplace

The president of a large business firm responded to a question about priorities in his life by saying, "On Sunday it is God first, family second, and business last. During the week the order is reversed." Most of us are not that candid, but examining a time log might force us to the same conclusion.

Ideally activities in work, worship, and family are complementary. Unfortunately in our society they compete for our limited available time.

Many jobs require commitments of time, energy, and travel that conflict with family needs. Children are neglected when parents do not have enough time to spend with them, or when both parents spend too much time away from home. Relationships at work can compete with family relationships. Some men and women spend more time with other people than they do with their spouses at home. This brings many temptations.

God established the family as one of the most important social institutions. It is important to nurture marriage relationships. The Bible speaks clearly of parents' responsibilities to love and care for their children (Deuteronomy 6:4–9; Luke 1:17; Titus 2:3–5). The Bible is less specific in indicating how this should be done.

One of the crucial challenges facing us is to find ways to resolve the conflicts between work and family. To do this we should more clearly define rights in the workplace that strengthen and support family life.

By 1987 fifteen states had laws relating to employee leaves of absence for pregnancy, birth, and postnatal care of children. Such benefits are well on the way toward being defined as employee rights. Some companies allow mothers to bring nursing babies along to work. More and more companies provide access to day-care facilities. Some provide such services themselves. Others contract with specialist agencies. Many companies provide referral services to assist parents in finding quality care for children.

Some companies are able to provide flexible working patterns that make it possible for parents to take children to the doctor or meet other needs that occur during working hours. One company allows mothers and fathers to use their personal paid sick leave to take care of sick children. Some positions are designed to allow two workers to share one job or to receive full health and retirement benefits in a part-time job. Computers enable some jobs to be done at home. All of these policies help make it possible to balance family and business obligations.

Because God considers family relationships important, we should support rights in the workplace that reinforce the development of strong families. Creative thought and research must be done to determine what programs and provisions employees should expect from their employers. We have come to identify payment of social security and health benefits as rights. Should things such as maternity and paternity leave, child care, flexible working schedules, or provision for nursing babies be considered rights?

Not everyone agrees that these policies strengthen family life. Some argue that they encourage parents to avoid their responsibilities. This concern raises a particularly important issue for families in our society: how to set priorities between family and work.

One of the myths that pervades our society is that "we can have it all." That is not true. There is not enough time and energy to do everything that is good. Pursuing a career often requires long hours and single-minded purpose. Little time and energy is left for family and church. Priority choices need to be made between work, family, community, church, recreation, personal time, and social life. Often church and family are the first to suffer. These priorities are particularly hard to set when both parents work away from home.

Both parents may work away from home for any number of reasons. Some feel a call to serve society or the church through an outside job. Taking time off from a career often retards advancement. Child care does not have the status of other jobs. Some want and need the fulfillment that comes from working away from home. Others have chosen a lifestyle that requires two incomes.

Many Christians have found that both parents can work away from home and still fulfill their responsibilities to their families. This requires hard choices. Sacrifices will need to be made at various points both in the career and in the family.

Some other Christians feel they should resist the pressure for both parents to work outside the home because of their understanding of biblical teaching. This allows one parent to give full attention to family life. Families must decide which parent takes this responsibility.

Unfortunately, because of economic demands, many families do not even have an option. Today the majority of working women are either single parents, widowed, or married to men with incomes too low to adequately support their families. These women must have an income to survive, and they desperately need their employer's help in balancing the demand of their families and paid employment.

This issue provides important challenges to Christian businesspersons. We should take leadership in finding creative and innovative approaches for providing quality care for families and protecting family rights affected by the workplace. We should begin by discussing the concerns our employees have about family life. Such discussions may lead to redesigned jobs, flexible working hours, policies that allow for shared jobs, varieties in benefit packages, or revised time-off policies. Such changes will take time and effort, but we cannot ignore the need to build up the family life of employees.

Brenda and Joe demonstrate one creative approach to balancing family and career. They have two children, one only a few months old. Although they are both nurses, Brenda is a college teacher and Joe works in a hospital. For the year following the birth of their new daughter they will share a half-time teaching job at the college where Brenda taught full time before. Brenda will teach nine hours and Joe three. Because this is half-time, Brenda can hold her position. She is also eligible for benefits such as health and retirement. She can spend more time at home. Joe also reduced his time at the hospital in order to be home more, though he continues at more than half-time. In addition they have hired a lovely "grandmother" neighbor to take care of the children when both need to be gone.

They have made some trade-offs. Their income is reduced because neither is working full time. They have sacrificed, at least for a time, some possibilities for career advancement. But they are maintaining their jobs and contributing significantly through them. Neither is at home with the children full time, but they are available much more than if they both worked full time. In addition the children have the advantage of learning to know an older person in their community to replace their own grandmother, who lives further away.

Employee Assistance Programs

John was the business manager of a Christian college. One of the employees in the physical plant began to miss work rather regularly. This continued even after several warnings. Policy would have dictated that he be fired. But in some of their conversations John discovered that the reason his work attendance was not satisfactory was his addiction to alcohol. Instead of getting rid of him, which would have been the easiest solution, John worked with the employee to develop a plan of treatment and counseling oriented toward finding release from the addiction. This went beyond the requirements of the policy. Unfortunately even after a year of the treatment the abuse continued and John was forced to release the employee.

An increasing number of people come to work with such debilitating personal problems. Many of these, such as alcoholism, drug dependency, or lung disease from smoking, result from wrong choices. The responsibility for other personal problems, such as the effects of a broken home, depression, or mental illness, are harder to identify. All of these affect job performance.

Many businesses provide services to help employees change their behavior when that is possible, or to learn to cope with hurtful situations that cannot be changed. These range from programs to help employees lose weight to programs of in-depth counseling for psychiatric problems.

The need for business to be involved in these problems often reflects the failure of other social institutions—such as the family, the community, or the church—to deal with them successfully. Business involvement also arises from the fact that work cannot be disconnected from other aspects of life. For business these programs often more than pay for themselves because of increased levels of performance, decreased absenteeism, and other benefits to the companies.

It is important to determine whether access to these services is an employee right. Are companies obligated to provide them? Business certainly does have obligations to the "person at work." The extent of obligations in more personal problem areas is not as clear. It is possible for business to "meddle" too much in the personal lives of employees. This may make problems worse. We may intrude on privacy. These services are also expensive. They will eventually increase product costs to customers. Yet customers should be willing to pay more for products from companies that take responsibilities toward their employees seriously.

The cost of these services puts firms that provide them at a competitive disadvantage compared to those who do not offer them, at least in the short run. Should these services then be mandated by the law or left to the discretion of individual companies? Making them legal mandates takes away the competitive advantage of firms that do not provide them. Yet many of us would worry about the complexity of resulting government regulations.

At this point we need to determine criteria for what services we will offer. Legally we have discretion, but we are still "our brother's keeper." We can use both humanitarian and economic criteria. We can also make distinctions between problems caused by wrong choices and those over which the employee has little control. We will make different choices about what assistance we provide; but it is important to clarify our obligations and limits in regard to employees' personal problems.

One Christian owner of a construction company that specialized in building churches wondered whether he should intervene with an employee who was psychologically depressed. Finally, after great deliberation, he called the employee in and offered to pay up to $2,000 for psychiatric help. The owner did not know what the outcome would be; but he believed he should offer help, since no one else seemed to be providing it. Now, several years later, the employee is well and still with the company. The employee has showed his gratitude through loyal committed service ever since. This offer of help created a bond of trust far beyond typical employer/employee relationships. This is the bond and trust we should strive for as Christians.

Medical Benefits

When businesspeople are asked to identify challenging personnel issues, most will list medical benefits near the top. The United States, in contrast to many other countries, has no broad plan providing for medical needs. Most people get medical insurance through their jobs. Access to medical coverage as a fringe benefit has been accepted by many people as an employee right.

There are many questions about which approaches provide the best coverage at the most reasonable rates. When medical coverage is linked to jobs, many unemployed and partially employed people will not have coverage. Costs are rising at phenomenal rates. We face particularly difficult problems providing medical care for employees who make lifestyle choices that increase medical risks. Examples include people who are overweight, abusers of alcohol and tobacco, even motorcycle riders. Statistically these persons are more vulnerable to infections, lung cancer, and accidents.

Businesses do not want to discriminate against groups with particularly high medical risks, such as the handicapped or older people. Yet hiring these groups often increases costs because of their special needs. Is it fair to ask a small business to carry those costs? Should insurance companies be allowed to charge higher rates for persons whose lifestyle choices increase risk?

Some form of medical coverage is seen by many people as a basic employee right. In fact a lack of any employer provision can quickly lead to destitution when accidents and illness occur. We should cooperate with our employees to fund basic medical protection for our work force. Finding ways to deliver quality medical coverage at reasonable cost deserves some of the best analysis and creative thinking that is available. We must work diligently in cooperation with our employees to find workable solutions to the issues of coverage and cost.

The Right to Privacy

The tensions between an employee's desire for privacy and an employer's need for information are substantial. Our Point for Discussion illustrates one example in which information on drug use can be constructively used or destructively abused. The union worries that random drug testing will violate employee privacy. The employer, Kerr-McGee, believes information on abusers will improve society. Another example, one of the most rapidly expanding benefits offered by business, is adolescent mental health care for the children of employees. The information gathered in providing this benefit must be handled very carefully and in confidence. Many employers keep knowledge of who uses various employee assistance programs confidential because it could be misused. In many companies not even the personnel director is told who goes for company paid counseling.

Even though privacy issues have been discussed intensely for some time, there are still a number of unresolved concerns. Christians should bring their perspectives to society's debate as well as to decisions in their jobs and businesses. Religious preference, family plans, alcohol use, mental or physical illness, drug use, convictions for crimes, and personal morality do have significant impact on job performance, but inquiry into them is limited by law. Employers frequently use honesty and lie detector tests to protect themselves. These too bring the conflict between an employer's need to know and an employee's rights of privacy into sharp focus.

Making sense of the many claims regarding human obligations and rights is a gigantic task. The social contract that defines rights and obligations is constantly changing in response to new situations and opportunities. The Bible does not give specific answers to many of these issues. At times cultural mores support biblical principles and at other times they contradict them. As we grapple with today's complex social issues, we need to be well grounded in the biblical principles of justice and love. Then we must pray for discernment as we seek to translate these principles into policies and actions in the workplace.

QUESTIONS FOR REFLECTION

Striking Over Drug Testing

1. At Kerr-McGee, what rights and obligations were in conflict? Are these issues of legal or moral rights and obligations?
2. What are the sources for the employer's and employee's notions of obligations and rights in this situation? Where should our basic sense about these concepts originate?

Exploring the Bible

1. Read Deuteronomy 24:14–16. What does this passage say about fair compensation? Should indirect benefits such as health insurance or child care be considered as part of fair compensation? Or simply as part of a strategy to attract and retain good employees?
2. Read Romans 7:14–25. How can Paul's comment on the nature of sin inform this discussion on defining rights and responsibilities?
3. Read 1 Corinthians 6:1–8. How should Christians handle a dispute about rights in the workplace both as employees and as employers?

Contemporary Comment

1. Review your job experience. Have you ever been in a situation where you felt your rights were violated? How did you react? Was your employer sensitive to your concerns?
2. Why are family rights in the workplace a more pressing issue today than they were twenty years ago? Should social change affect an employer's obligations?

3. If employees believe they have a right to medical benefits, what corresponding obligation might be placed on employees?
4. Should employers take the initiative to build opportunities for employees to exercise their rights, by building avenues of appeal when individual rights such as privacy are threatened?
5. Max DePree, former president of Herman Miller, Inc., a manufacturer of fine furniture, suggests the following rights of workers. Do you agree that all of these are rights? Are there others? What policies would you establish to implement these?

- The right to be needed
- The right to be involved
- The right to a covenant relationship
- The right to understand
- The right to affect one's own destiny
- The right to be accountable
- The right to appeal

NOTES

1. *The Grand Rapids Press* (December 11, 1987). Grand Rapids, MI. Associated Press News Features Service. Used with permission.
2. Paul Marshall, "I Have Rights, Don't I," *The Banner* (March 7, 1988): 13, CRC Publications, Grand Rapids, MI.

Chapter 10

PLANNING AND ORGANIZING: MEANS OF DOING JUSTICE

<small>POINT FOR DISCUSSION</small>

God's Plan . . . for What?

"Because God does have plans for organizations and individuals, some people use this as a cop-out for not planning. The chairman of one church board told me he thought it was a sin to plan. 'Why plan?' he asked. 'I know God is in control, so I'm just trusting Him.'

My question is, 'For what?'

On the other hand, some Christian leaders feel they must do it all. They not only plan every detail, but also think they must produce the results. There is no place for this type of thinking in a Christian organization. Paul makes this point clear by saying, 'I planted the seed, Apollos watered it, but God made it grow' (1 Corinthians 3:6).

The Christian leader must realize his job is to determine the actions God wants him to take and then trust God for the results. As the Bible says again, 'Many are the plans in a man's heart, but it is the Lord's purpose that prevails' " (Proverbs 19:21).[1]

Why Plan?

Planning is important for Christians in business because it helps us achieve justice. Justice does not happen automatically. It cannot exist apart from very careful planning. Because there are many pressures that drag an organization toward unethical conduct, there must be constant effort to keep it on target. We must work hard to plan to do what is right in products, services, prices, wages, dividends, and all other areas of business. Thoughtful planning helps us to monitor our motives and actions at every turn. Justice is not merely wanting to do what is right but actually doing what is right. A good planning process can help this happen.

Look at the diagram below. The horizontal axis represents time. The vertical axis distance between the lines represents the range of decision possibilities available to the decision maker. The further apart the lines the greater number of options are available. At the right end is the point when a decision must be made.

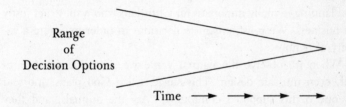

This simple diagram suggests that the closer you get to the point where you need to make a decision, the fewer options are available. Planning is a way of anticipating decisions early so that a large number of options are available, both to the organization and to the individuals involved.

The board members of a small college decided in the middle of June that enrollment would drop for the following fall. This meant they had too many faculty members and would need to release several if they were to balance their budget. Contracts were to take effect on July 1. They decided not to offer contracts to several faculty who were planning to teach that fall. In early June one of those teachers had turned down an offer from a local high school because she had a job at the college. After July 1 there were no other teaching jobs available in that community, so that fall she was unemployed.

Many people in the community felt the college's decision was unjust. Was it?

In June, several weeks before the contracts began, there was nothing else they could do. They were limited to terminating teachers after all other teaching jobs in the community were filled, or running a deficit in their budget. But back in January figures were available that indicated enrollment would drop. Had they thought about the future at this time, many more options would have been available. The college could have tried harder to recruit students. The teachers who were cut could have looked for and probably found other jobs. Teachers could have taken other assignments within the college. The college's lack of planning resulted in a decision that treated some people unfairly.

Planning is vitally important for Christians who want to act justly in business. We must anticipate decisions in order to ensure a variety of options.

When we observe the natural world we see evidence of careful, even intricate design. This suggests that God plans. Job said to one of his supposed comforters, "Ask the animals, and they will teach you, or the birds . . . and they will tell you . . . let the fish of the sea inform you . . . that the hand of the Lord has done this" (Job 12:7-9).

Many scientists recognize God's planning in nature. Recently a British scientist asserted that the mathematical probability of a tornado passing through a junk yard and assembling a Boeing 747 from the scrap heap is far greater than the probability that the universe came into being without a sovereign creator.

The Bible also reveals God's planning through many examples of fulfilled prophecy.

God has created animals and people with the capacity to prepare for the future. The monarch butterfly migrates with the seasons over thousands of miles; Canadian geese plot their way over long distances. Ants gather and store food. What animals do by instinct, people do with conscious and directed effort. We are able to analyze and understand events and make meaningful decisions that will guide our response.

Jesus illustrated this when he said,

> When you see a cloud rising in the west, immediately you say, "A shower is coming," and so it turns out. And when you see a south wind blowing, you say, "It will be a hot day," and it turns out that way. You hypocrites! You know how to analyze the appearance of the earth and the sky, but why do you not analyze this present time? (Luke 12:54–56 NASB)

The people were able to interpret the weather, but were unable or unwilling to really understand what was happening in their social and political world. Christ realized that we sometimes fail to see the really important things that should help us determine our actions.

Matching Our Plans with God's

Only God has perfect and certain knowledge of the future. Nonetheless we expend great energy trying to forecast the future. We extrapolate events, project trends, examine signs, analyze changes, build economic models, and make guesses in an effort to prepare for or shape what is likely to happen in the future. Both our ability to predict the future and our knowledge about the effects of our decisions, however, are limited.

The Bible warns us about the limitations of our knowledge. It is rather arrogant for us to think we know more than we do. After all, God is the only one who knows the past and the future. Our planning must always be done with the understanding that we are finite. The following Scriptures contrast God's sovereignty with our limitations.

> The mind of man plans his way, but the Lord directs his steps. (Proverbs 16:9 NASB)
> A plan in the heart of a man is like deep water, but a man of understanding draws it out. (Proverbs 20:5 NASB)

Come now, you who say, "Today or tomorrow, we shall go to such and such a city, and spend a year there and engage in business and make a profit." Yet you do not know what your life will be like tomorrow . . . Instead, you ought to say, "If the Lord wills, we shall live and also do this or that." But as it is you boast in your arrogance; all such boasting is evil. (James 4:13–16 NASB)

These passages suggest that God ultimately determines what will happen. In spite of God's sovereignty and control of the world, however, we are to make plans and carry them out. That is one of the paradoxes we find hard to understand. God is in control, yet we make decisions that really make a difference. Our calling and task is to know God's will so well that we can make our plans in complete harmony with God's will and plan. All of our plans are made within a much larger master plan. In a very real sense God is the sovereign planner, and we are subplanners.

We acknowledge up front that our abilities to plan are limited. So why should we plan in business at all? Because good stewardship and our concerns for justice demand it. Planning is an effort not so much to control outcomes, but to increase options for action and to reduce unnecessary risks. We are God's moral agents, who are confronted constantly with choices between competing values and alternative uses of resources. We must make plans to help us sift through and select those options that assist us in matching our objectives to God's goals for his world.

A Good Planning Process

A good planning process includes a balance between leadership from the top of the organization and involvement from the bottom. We should be sensitive to the need for members of the organization to participate in formulating the plans they will implement. Employees must have ownership in plans if they are to be expected to work with them. Employees should be allowed to willingly accept their role as it fits within the business plan.

One of the most frequent causes of ineffective planning is plans that do not include implementation steps. A good plan includes identification of how policies will be changed, personnel recruited, and corporate culture managed in order to implement the plan. Therefore planning is not a one-time act. It is an ongoing process of adjusting, refining, assessing, and decision making.

Common sense tells us it is good to involve people in the planning process at the point that the plan affects their work. When those responsible for carrying out a plan are excluded from its development, they will have neither the motivation nor the information to adjust and implement the plan effectively.

It also makes sense to include a broad range of people in the planning process. Talents, knowledge, and understanding are dispersed across the entire community of participants in business.

We must seek counsel from many business participants if we are to make sound plans. Solomon declared, "Through presumption comes nothing but strife [failure], but with those who receive counsel is wisdom" (Proverbs 13:10 NASB). People who presume they have sufficient knowledge in themselves often create many problems, and solve few. "The way of a fool seems right to him, but a wise man listens to advice" (Proverbs 12:15). Planning is deciding on a course of action. It should involve counsel and participation by those involved. Doing justice—doing what is right—requires good planning that involves everyone in the business and that is based on broad counsel and advice.

Models for Organizational Structure

Organizational structures are formed to implement plans. They help us explore, produce, market, distribute, and serve customers. They organize many support functions—finance, accounting, information systems, personnel offices, and other staff and service groups—that assist the line operations involved in the creation and handling of business goods and services.

Structures are meant to serve people. Organizational structures, both the informal or formal ones, are nothing more than human relationships that have been defined as to authority, responsibility, accountability, policies, and procedures. No organization can exist without structure. Moses structured the policies and procedures to solve disputes among the Israelites. Nehemiah organized the work of Israel in rebuilding the walls of Jerusalem. Organizational structures formalize relationships to accomplish a group's purpose.

Structures That Serve Justice

God has a great interest in unity, harmony, and peace among diverse people created with a variety of talents and abilities (Ephesians 4:11–13). In a fallen world we need to structure ourselves in a manner that will enhance the harmonious use of God-given abilities.

There are many kinds of organizational structures: functional hierarchies like General Motors, participative teams like 3M, or matrix organizations like Proctor and Gamble. In addition to the formal structure, every organization has informal structure that emerges from the social interaction of the participants. Communication flows in both structures. People respond to formal controls in the formal structure, interpersonal controls in the informal structure, and to the self-control they have developed.

Implementing justice through organizational structures requires us to balance the need of freedom with the need for control, and the need for harmonious teamwork with the need for individual creativity and initiative (Galatians 5:13; 1 Corinthians 12:4–6). Organizational structures can assist or inhibit the proper balance of these competing needs.

Here are several principles for establishing organizational structures:

1. Develop structures that provide maximum freedom for every employee, based on their levels of maturity and commitment, as long as they work within the objectives of the organization. Decision making should be at the lowest level possible.
2. Create an environment that rewards individual creativity and initiative. Encourage employees to think of new and better ways of doing things.

3. Give rewards in ways that encourage group effort and cooperation between people and operational units. Rewards should also encourage workers to do what is best for the company in the long run, and not only what makes them look good in the short run.

4. Clearly identify responsibilities, lines of accountability, and communication patterns.

5. Develop structures that provide for interaction and collaboration between all people and groups involved in a project, even though they might be in different departments or divisions. They should facilitate good lateral communication.

6. Develop lean structures with as few hierarchical levels as possible.

We must always be aware of the tendency for organizations to become top-heavy bureaucracies and to develop rules and procedures that are dysfunctional. It is easy for members of organizations to divert their attention from reaching the goal and direct their efforts to careful following of all the rules instead. The story is told of a school librarian who was very proud of the good condition of the books in the library. She was able to report to her board that she seldom if ever needed to replace lost books and that her repair budget was very low. When asked how she accomplished this, she said that she never let children use the books. She had forgotten the real goal of a library and replaced it with a bureaucratic one.

This is not a criticism of all organizational procedures and rules. But it is important to recognize the tendency for traditions, forms, rituals, and customs to become constraints, blocks, and wastes of creative energy.

In the days of Christ many of the Pharisees piled traditions on top of God's law, all too frequently obscuring the spirit of the law. In the Sermon on the Mount in Matthew 5, Jesus repeatedly says, "You have heard that it was said . . ." He found it necessary to challenge human traditions that perverted God's intent. Similarly Christian business leaders should continuously review all structures and procedures to be certain that procedures serve the goals of the organization and the employees. A good structure will serve the people, and not the other way around.

An institution is doing justice with its business structure when that structure fosters a community capable of sustaining productive, satisfying, interdependent work relationships that enable individual workers to develop their talents to the fullest while providing quality goods and services. Structures should be designed to facilitate reaching these goals.

QUESTIONS FOR REFLECTION

God's Plan . . . for What?

1. What does God tell us about his plan for our work with natural revelation?
2. What kinds of things haven't been revealed?

Exploring the Bible

1. Read Matthew 6:25–34 and review James 4:13–16. Are these passages advising us against planning for personal and business situations? What is the appropriate role of planning? Should plans be open to change?
2. Read Exodus 18:13–26. Why does Jethro suggest a different organizational structure to Moses? Would such a structure effectively meet the needs of most contemporary businesses?
3. Read Romans 12:4–8. How can planning and organizational structure enable individuals with gifts to serve the good of the whole community?

Contemporary Comment

1. Comment on the following:

> Every good manager is a decision maker, a risk-taker. If your identity is tied up with the success of the business, you will inevitably be afraid of failure, restricting your ability to make bold decisions. A

Christian manager has the freedom to make those decisions because the central focus is on Christ. Your identity comes from your relationship with Christ and there is no need to be hung up about business failure.[2]

Should Christians be able to plan for greater levels of risk-taking in their business planning than non-Christians?

2. Why might Christian managers worry about losing control of the company's plans if they invite employees to participate in the planning process? Should they worry?

3. The authors suggest that a key criterion for appropriate organizational structure is how well it serves the people who work in the business. How could a structure that serves employees well *not* serve customers or stockholders effectively?

4. List your three most prominent personal gifts. Explain how you use them to serve others within some organization of which you are a member.

NOTES

1. Myron Rush, *Management: A Biblical Approach* (Wheaton, IL: Victor Books, 1983), 82. Copyright © 1983 SP Publications, Wheaton, IL. Reprinted by permission.
2. Dennis Bakke, executive vice president, Applied Energy Services. From John A. Bernbaum and Simon M. Steer, *Why Work?* (Grand Rapids, MI: Baker Book House, 1986), 65.

PART 3

Leadership: To Rule or to Serve?

Chapter 11

A CHRISTIAN CONCEPT OF LEADERSHIP

POINT FOR DISCUSSION

Mixing Faith and Business Leadership

Is it really possible to be a committed Christian and a committed corporate leader? Some Christians wonder whether business leadership can be consistent with true faith; but while they wonder, many other Christians strive to do just that—mix faith and business leadership.

Here's a sample of these Christians at work:

Name	Position
Wayne Alderson	Former Vice President for Operations, Pittron Steel; founder, Value of the Person
Betsy Ancker-Johnson	Vice President, General Motors
Dennis Bakke	Executive Vice President, Applied Energy Services
Clayton Brown	Owner and chief executive, Clayton Brown and Associates, municipal bonds brokers
Art DeFehr	President, Palliser Furniture Co.

Gary Ginter	Commodities Broker, Chicago Research and Trading
Anthony Rossi	Founder, Tropicana Products
Paul Pearson	Director of Human Resources Development, Steelcase Corp., Inc.
C. William Pollard	President, Service Master Industries, Inc.
William Walton	Co-founder, Holiday Inns, Inc.

All of these people are leaders in their industries. The position titles indicate their clout. Yet each of them is a Christian whom their peers describe with adjectives not always associated with business. Words such as "humble, fair, approachable, honest, peacemaker, idealist, and courageous" are often used. They are also cited as being "responsive, competitive, risk-taking, problem-solving, and brilliant strategists."

Each of these leaders makes a unique contribution. One emphasizes balance between business goals and the needs of society. Another gave millions to charity. A third quit the company when new policies challenged his moral values. A fourth works closely with non-Christian executives in his company.

All of these leaders share a common commitment. Each believes in Jesus as Savior and in the Bible as the source of values and conduct. Each has worked over many years to blend faith with business leadership. Each knows that non-Christians watch carefully to see if faith and business conduct can mesh successfully. Each has orchestrated the simultaneous concerns of employees, customers, and public policy.

They are all leaders. They are all Christians. Their faith affects their leadership as it does scores of other Christians in similar positions.

The Art of Leadership

Would you like to work for a boss described with such words as "loose cannon, incredibly impulsive, old blood-and-guts, really abusive, horrendous, towering temper, big ego"?[1] This is how *Fortune* described America's toughest bosses in an article by that title. Without casting judgment on the tough bosses, let's reflect on the impact of faith on leadership style.

Good business leadership is an art. It provides direction and purpose for an organization. It elicits trust and helps employees focus on the big purposes of the organization. Leadership must be earned. It is voluntarily given by those who follow, not taken by those who lead. Followers perceive that leaders can work with them to provide opportunities to meet their personal goals while making a contribution to the goals of the business.

Everyone is endowed with some leadership qualities. Not everyone is capable of being the chief executive officer of Exxon, of course, but each of us has the potential to lead in certain circumstances. Each of us can grow and develop leadership skills.

Character of Christian Leaders

Tropicana Products, under Anthony Rossi, grew to include a vast network of orange groves and processing plants. William Walton built the huge Holiday Inn franchise from scratch in a little over thirty years. Dennis Bakke's company is rapidly developing a name in the energy industry for good management practices and environmental responsibility. These people are getting results. They are also committed Christians.

Before we can look at what Christian leaders do, we must examine who they are. There are certain character traits that characterize Christian leaders. They are not different from the characteristics of all Christians. But it is important to see how these traits are expressed in leadership.

The Beatitudes in Matthew 5:3–9 can be used as a checklist of the inner personality characteristics of Christians. They describe a set of qualities that should be present in all Christians, especially leaders.

"Blessed are the poor in spirit, for theirs is the kingdom of heaven. Blessed are those who mourn, for they will be comforted" (Matthew 5:3–4). This could be rephrased to say, "Blessed are those who know how poor in spirit they really are." When we compare ourselves to Jesus Christ we become aware of how imperfect we really are. The contrast helps us recognize the depth and impact of our fallen nature.

Christian leaders are humble. They have a realistic understanding of their skills and abilities and understand that these are given to them by God. Such leaders who are "poor in spirit" are not defensive. They understand their own weaknesses. Because of that, they can be open and vulnerable. They accept and welcome constructive counsel from superiors, colleagues, and subordinates. They realize that they are strengthened by the teamwork of others.

Humble leaders are also acutely aware of how they often fall short of their own best intentions and the high purposes of God. They "mourn" over how far from God's ways they are. Such leaders are not like Charles Dickens's Uriah Heep, who walked around with a long face, groaning, "Oh, woe is me." They do not degrade themselves, but are aware of their limitations. They are open to criticism and learn from it. They recognize their dependence on God, their superiors, their followers, and their peers.

This humility frees leaders from some of the actions that prevent leaders from being effective. They do not need to hold on to power or false status. They can build strong teams that use the skills of many persons, some even stronger than they are themselves. They are not afraid to delegate, and they are always learning and growing.

Victor was the owner and president of a large food processing firm in eastern Pennsylvania grossing several hundred million dollars a year. An article in a local newspaper described what happened at an annual company dinner. As the guests were being seated, Victor approached one of the tables with several empty seats. In his usual humble, unassuming way, he quietly asked if it was all right for him to sit there. That kind of humility characterized all of his business relationships.

"Blessed are the meek, for they will inherit the earth" (Matthew 5:5). Meekness is also a characteristic of Christian leaders. It flows naturally from true humility. While humility acknowledges weakness, meekness acknowledges the strength of gentleness. Compare the words used to describe the tough bosses in the opening paragraph with the words used to describe the businesspeople in the Point for Discussion. The tough bosses rely on threats and force. The article says, "They could scare cream into butter and make money in the deal."

As a horse responds to the reins of the rider, the meek respond to the will of God. The horse's spirit is not broken when it is bridled. Similarly a Christian leader's personality, drive, energy, and creativity are not negated when submitted to God's will. The Christian leader relates to people with gentleness and meekness, not arrogance and pride. Both Jesus and Moses are examples of powerful leaders who used the power of meekness.

"Blessed are those who hunger and thirst for righteousness, for they will be filled" (Matthew 5:6). Have you ever gone for a long period without food or water? Remember how your every thought was related to food and drink? That is how Christians are to live their lives, thinking continually about righteousness and justice. In business we are called to have a singleminded drive to find ways to practice justice. It is first a hungering for Christ, which subsequently grows into a longing for justice in the marketplace. A Christian business leader should be consumed by a desire to live righteously and do justice.

"Blessed are the merciful, for they will be shown mercy" (Matthew 5:7). The key expression of mercy is forgiveness. Leaders have many opportunities to show mercy and forgiveness. We must begin by learning to forgive ourselves. Leaders make a lot of decisions, and consequently a lot of mistakes. So we need to find ways of accepting forgiveness from others and from God when we do make errors in judgment that hurt other people.

We are also invited to be understanding and forgiving of people with whom we work. That does not mean we should overlook mistakes or wrong acts or poor performance. Rather we should deal with them in ways that encourage people to learn from mistakes and improve. A story is told of a former president of a large computer company. A young employee made a mistake that cost the company several million dollars. He approached the president, prepared for the worst. To make matters easier, he offered his resignation. The president said that he would not accept the resignation, since it had just cost the company several million dollars to educate the man and they were not about to let him go! That was the president's way of showing mercy.

Thomas Edison had spent thousands of hours developing an incandescent light bulb. He gave it to a young assistant to carry upstairs. As he reached the top stair he tripped and pieces of the shattered bulb scattered all over the floor. Edison began immediately to build another. When it was finished he called the young assistant, handed the bulb to him, and asked him to carry it upstairs. There was nothing more effective that Edison could have done to show that he was ready to forget the unfortunate incident and move on. That kind of action rebuilds confidence. You can be sure that young man was a loyal and trusted employee who could be counted on to do his best in the future.

When we show mercy to others, they in turn show mercy to us. Leaders who do not forgive mistakes will be judged harshly by the people who work with them.

"Blessed are the pure in heart, for they will see God" (Matthew 5:8). Christian leaders should become purer and purer in heart as they continue to grow more like Christ. They should become less and less double-minded, with fewer and fewer contradictions between their profession of faith and their daily conduct. Such leaders behave more consistently in a Christlike way. They do right not only when it is profitable, but even when it is costly. They do not act from mixed motives. Purity in heart comes to assume a more important place than the next promotion, the bottom line, or the embarrassment of full disclosure. The pure in heart live on a single track with clear pure motives, pursuing righteousness.

"Blessed are the peacemakers, for they will be called sons of God" (Matthew 5:9). Christian business leaders will grow in their ability to become peacemakers who foster unity, cooperation, teamwork, and reconciliation. During difficult disagreements they try to find solutions in which all can gain. We do not seek peace at any price, at the expense of justice and righteousness; rather we seek strategies of reconciliation, and cooperation whenever possible.

This list in no way exhausts the characteristics of Christian leaders. Galatians 5:22–24 lists the fruits of the spirit—love, joy, peace, patience, kindness, goodness, faithfulness, gentleness, and self-control. These too give very practical directions for leaders. The inner strength of Christian leaders is absolutely essential to faithful Christian leadership.

Responsibilities of Christian Leaders

It is important for leaders to develop inner strength and character. They must reflect very seriously on the special responsibilities of leaders and the special shape given to those responsibilities by faith. The list below is certainly not comprehensive, but it does suggest some starting points.

1. *Christian business leaders are models of moral behavior.* They should themselves live out the values that are essential to healthy organizations. They should represent the character, drive, capability, opportunity, and integrity of the business. To a considerable degree they symbolize the organization to their subordinates. Lee Iacocca is an example of a leader who became the symbol of the value of quality to the employees and customers of Chrysler.

   Often a tougher standard is applied to Christians in business than is applied to others. Observers who know a leader is a dedicated Christian will generally expect that person to act differently. Actions such as rude conduct, coarse language, or sexist attitudes might be tolerated in some people, but would be hypocritical if practiced by Christians.

This role as model was already established in the Old Testament. The prophet Nathan confronted King David following his adulterous relationship with Bathsheba and said, "By this deed you have given occasion to the enemies of the Lord to blaspheme . . ." (2 Samuel 12:14 NASB). By his conduct David opened the door for people to scoff at the Lord and show contempt. Today many people still attempt to justify their own immoral conduct by citing the inconsistencies of Christian leaders.

Departments and organizations reflect characteristics of their leaders. The director of admissions at a small Christian college has a rare sense of humor and quick wit. All over campus that department is known as a department where people have fun. Even now that the director has been promoted the department has the most hilarious birthday celebrations on campus. The director's style and pattern of conduct is mirrored by the department members. This is true in other areas too. The values of a department and organization reflect those modeled by their leaders, such as whether they tend to be punctual or late, patient or impatient, diligent or slack.

This is equally true in ethical matters. When a leader tends to pad expense accounts or renege on agreements or shade the truth, those values will pervade the organization. Followers have little incentive to rise above the standards and qualities embodied in their leaders. Leaders have a responsibility to set a high moral tone for the business.

2. *Leaders are responsible to articulate and carry the vision for the organization.* Leaders keep activity focused on the purpose of the organization. They help employees find meaning in their work. Scripture states, "Where there is no vision, the people are unrestrained" (Proverbs 29:18 NASB). They have no direction; they founder and seem at loose ends and they drift. Leaders are expected to remind employees of the vision that gives their work purpose and direction.

Christian business leaders must believe in the rightness of the organization's goals. For example, CMDS president Dwight Wyse, whose purpose was cited in the Point for Discussion in Chapter 1, continually reminds members of the firm of the purpose by talking about it, using it in prominent places in advertising, and by using it to orient new employees.

3. *Leaders are responsible to maintain open communication.* Employees look to leaders to keep them informed and to provide them with the information they need to do their job effectively. Warren Braun, president of Comsonics in Virginia, feels that it is every employee's right to know a great deal about the financial status of the company. His company sponsored classes taught by a professor from a nearby college on accounting and reading financial statements. Not only did he make information available, he helped employees gain the skill to understand and interpret it.

Honesty in communication is one of the characteristics of Christian leaders. The Bible says, "Simply let your 'yes' be 'yes' and your 'no' 'no'; anything beyond this comes from the evil one" (Matthew 5:37). There is information that leaders cannot share because of its confidentiality or because it might injure other persons. But apart from that, communication should be clear, simple, unambiguous, and to the point. It should not be necessary to read between the lines to know what a Christian leader is saying.

4. *Christian leaders are responsible for team building.* At the center of smoothly functioning teams is a high level of trust. This means that members of the firm will know that they will be rewarded for cooperating with others for the good of the organization, even though it may seem to reduce their own production. And they should be rewarded for making decisions that serve the long-term interests of the organization, even at some short-term cost.

For example, grading systems in college that are based on the curve do not encourage students to collaborate or help each other. Students who understand the system know that it is not in their self-interest to help another student get a good grade since that might lower their own. A medical doctor tells how some of his classmates in medical school actually contaminated their classmates' lab experiments to lower the curve.

There are many management approaches to encourage trust and teamwork. People can be rewarded because of their contribution to a group rather than for their individual effort. Long-term results can be emphasized in evaluating employees.

5. *Christian leaders are responsible to create environments that encourage and facilitate growth and creativity.* Peter Drucker, author of many books and articles on management and a consultant to many of America's largest companies, suggests in a management training film that one of the primary tasks of leaders is to remove obstacles to performance. Unnecessary red tape and bureaucracy impede good performance. Decisions that need to move through unnecessary levels are often delayed, which in turn reduces productivity. Employees who are not given authority to make decisions are limited in their growth toward responsibility.

Some organizational environments support motivation; others stifle it. Leaders can energize an environment. By their enthusiasm and sheer competence they can release the life, vitality, drive, and spirit of the people with whom they work.

6. *Leaders must also manage the functions and procedures of an organization.* They are responsible to see that the day-to-day decisions get made. Someone must finally be responsible for the who, what, when, where, and how.

Good Followers

Leadership is important, but no one can be a good leader without good followers. Although some of us will end up in leadership positions, all of us will be followers. Therefore it is just as important to develop the skills of following as it is to develop skills of leading.

William Crockett, in an article in *Industry Week*, said that good followers "are not corporate sheep who are sheared every day, nor are they quiet submissive peons. Good followers are people who respond creatively to leadership and who are productive, creative members of a team." He identified a number of characteristics that make good followers:

1. Good followers create a climate of win/win situations with the boss so that there is little feeling of competition.
2. Good followers have enough self-confidence to challenge the boss and be a loyal "devil's advocate."
3. Good followers obey the boss's orders yet they do not become subservient.
4. Good followers happily fit their own particular skills and experience into the team without competing for the roles of other team members.
5. Good followers are loyal to the boss and to the goals of the team, while retaining the ability to be reflective and constructively critical.
6. Good followers leave when it becomes apparent that they no longer can support the values and goals of the organization or the boss.[2]

We can be good leaders only if we have first learned to be good followers. It is important that leaders always understand the position of followers.

The Principle of Balance

Most decisions leaders make do not pit one alternative that is right against one that is wrong. All alternatives have both good and not-so-good points. The leader needs to weigh all the factors and choose the one that seems to be the best for that situation. For this reason leaders need to be concerned about the principle of balance. The concept of balance is not to be equated with always seeking consensus or being in the middle of the road. Nor does it mean doing a little bit of this and a little of that. Balance points to the proper weighing and inclusion of all information, all viewpoints, and all conflicts in arriving at a sound judgment.

We often tend to focus on one good thing and become so absorbed with it that we forget to consider balancing realities. Our narrow emphasis sometimes offends people with a different perspective. We need to remind ourselves that other viewpoints are often healthy correctives to our own.

For example, envision a flat circular disk, six feet in diameter, pivoting on one point in the center. On the edges of the disk, ninety degrees apart, place equal weights representing "control," "freedom," "management," and "servanthood." Now envision yourself standing on the disk. Your job is to keep it balanced while it rotates. Periodically someone throws, at random, two- to five-pound sandbags on the disk. You need considerable mental concentration and dexterity to keep this disk in balance.

It takes wisdom for leaders to strike a proper balance between placing controls on employees and providing freedom which releases them to be creative. A purchasing agent needs to be given discretion to decide what gifts to accept from suppliers. Yet, if she has no guidelines, she may develop improper obligations to the gift givers.

Some controls need to be placed on the employees who write checks in accounts payable. Yet if there are too many controls they will become inefficient and unproductive. The personnel manager of an assembly line decided that employees were taking too many breaks to go to the bathroom. He suspected that they were actually going to the restroom to smoke. In order to correct that abuse he instituted a system of passes. Each employee was required to request a bathroom pass from the supervisor in order to leave the line to use the restroom. Only two passes were available. Employees felt that they were being treated like children, and they responded by going on strike. The manager could have found a reasonable solution if he had sought a balance between the extremes of having no coordination on restroom breaks and the pass system, by involving the employees. His extreme response set off a costly strike.

We must find the same balance between directing and serving. Directing suggests telling people what to do, setting deadlines, and in general giving orders. Serving suggests guiding, teaching, and assisting. Good leaders do both. They learn how to adjust their approach to the needs of their employees. Employees with less motivation and skill respond best to management that is directive and "tell" oriented. Employees with high motivation and skill levels respond best to suggestions and general directions.

Leaders manage and serve only by the consent of those managed. An effective leader needs to be trusted by those whom he or she attempts to lead. In the final analysis people manage themselves at the leader's request.

Leaders not only need knowledge, they need wisdom to see how the people and pieces of the business interact. This comes from long experience and from integrating the Scripture into our lives. David said, "Thy commandments make me wiser than my enemies, for they are ever mine. I have more insight than all my teachers, for Thy testimonies are my meditation. I understand more than the aged, because I have observed Thy precepts" (Psalms 119:98–100 NASB).

Christian leaders also find great help and reinforcement through their fellowship with other Christians. When they are struggling with heavy moral decisions many business leaders turn to their Church, the organized Body of Christ. This may involve counseling with their pastor or with another Christian businessperson. Many join associations of Christian businesspersons where they can find help and wise counsel. Others find help in reading good books. Interaction with other Christians can help us develop the inner Christian character required for business leadership. They can assist us in developing wise responses to carry the difficult weights of leadership.

As a conclusion to this chapter let's look at several questions that leaders can use to test the quality of their leadership:

- Do the people I lead grow and develop their skills?
- Do they grow in their ability to make decisions and take responsibility?
- Do they learn to collaborate more with their coworkers?
- Do they participate in decision making?
- Do they feel supported and challenged?
- Do they become better, more productive people under my leadership?

If the answers are yes, you are a good leader.

QUESTIONS FOR REFLECTION

Mixing Faith and Business Leadership

1. Name other Christian business leaders in your community or nation with whom you identify.
2. What makes them effective as Christian leaders and as businesspeople?

Exploring the Bible

1. Read Exodus 3:1–14 and 4:10–16. Do we sometimes try to excuse ourselves from leadership responsibilities, as did Moses? How did God promise to support Moses in leading Israel? In what ways does God support Christian leaders today?
2. Read John 13:12–17 and Luke 22:24–27. How do these passages reinforce our understanding of Christian leaders as servants? Who do these leaders serve?
3. Read Galatians 5:22–23. Trait theories of leadership list a series of attributes that make someone a successful leader. Should Christians replace that trait list with the fruits of the Spirit?

Contemporary Comment

1. The authors suggest that Christian business leaders are important as symbolic models. Will Christian leaders be held to

higher standards of behavior than non-Christians? How do non-Christians react to Christian leaders who fail either personally or professionally?

2. Max DePree wrote:

> Organization charts usually picture the leader at the top, with meaningful interaction flowing primarily downward. I would like to suggest that the structure should be an inverted triangle, showing the roots as the basis of leadership in the serving posture and demonstrating that an organization builds on its base or from its roots.[3]

If we Christians see leaders as the bottom of an inverted triangle of employees, what difference does it make?

3. Textbooks discuss two types of leadership styles, task-oriented and employee- (relationship-) oriented. The task-oriented leader focuses on working with and through people to be efficient and productive. The employee-oriented leader focuses on employees' happiness, satisfaction, and personal needs. Discuss whether both styles can be Christian.

4. Some leaders don't lead. What would be a Christian way to handle ineffective leaders?

NOTES

1. Peter Nulty, "America's Toughest Bosses," *Fortune* (February 27, 1989): 40–51.
2. William Crockett, "How to Be a Good Follower," *Industry Week* (November 15, 1976).
3. Max DePree, "The Process of Work: Is This a Brother Keeping Business?" *The Reformed Journal* (May 1979): 9–13. Published by Wm. B. Eerdmans, Grand Rapids, MI.

Chapter 12

THE CHRISTIAN'S USE OF POWER

How Would Jesus Respond to This?

"All life is a game of power. The object of the game is simple enough: to know what you want and get it. The moves of the game, by contrast, are infinite and complex, although they usually involve the manipulation of people and situations to your advantage. As for the rules, these are only discovered by playing the game to the end . . .

"No matter who you are, the basic truth is that your interests are nobody else's concern, your gain is inevitably someone else's loss, your failure someone else's victory. In the words of Henrich von Treitscheke, the German philosopher of might, 'Your neighbor, even though he may look upon you as his natural ally against another power which is feared by you both, is always ready, at the first opportunity, as soon as it can be done with safety, to better himself at your expense . . . Whoever fails to increase his power, must decrease it, if others increase theirs.' "[1]

The Danger of Power

In September 1989 PTL leader Jim Bakker was convicted of twenty-one counts of defrauding people. Jim and his wife, Tammy, were gifted with the ability to inspire people to follow them and to invest large sums of money in their projects. They built a huge Christian televangelism empire, a theme park, and a resort community. They had tremendous power and used it to minister to many people.

But Jim and Tammy Bakker found out how dangerous power can be. They began to use their power to live an extravagant lifestyle. They built an air-conditioned dog house. They liked the smell of cinnamon buns, so they had several hundred delivered to their hotel room. Several days later they threw all of them away without eating any. They promised lifetime use of guestrooms in their resort hotel to people who gave contributions, but made that promise to many times the number of people who could be accommodated. They let power corrupt them. They could have used it to serve others; instead they used it to deceive others and to benefit themselves.

The story of Jim and Tammy Bakker would make it seem that power is evil and the use of power wrong. Not so. Power is the ability to get things done. Without the exercise of power nothing could get done. Moses used God's power to lead the people of Israel out of slavery. Milton Hershey, the founder of the Hershey chocolate company, used power and money to serve thousands of children who had lost one of their parents by providing foster homes and a school. This ministry continues through a foundation that owns a majority of Hershey stock. Charles Colson gained a lot of power through his high position as an adviser to President Nixon. Before his conversion he used that power to hurt people in his attempts to bolster the position of the president. After his conversion he used it to build a far-reaching ministry to prisoners and to influence many national and international leaders to follow Christ.

The appropriate use of power is necessary to get anything done. Yet power has the ability to seduce people. Scripture tells us we are born with a tendency to sin (Psalms 51:5; 58:3), and in business this often expresses itself in the misuse of power. In 1889 Lord Acton wrote, "Power tends to corrupt and absolute power corrupts absolutely."

There are many ways power can be used wrongly: to thwart the valid concerns of coworkers, to protect our jobs, to gain personal advantage. Power might be used to bolster our bid for a higher rung in the ladder of success. We can be tempted to be dishonest in order to gain more power. Stock traders who use insider tips do so to gain an advantage over their competitors in making stock transactions. Business power is dangerous because of the traps it opens. It is as intoxicating and addictive to some people as alcohol and drugs are to others. It has the same capacity for self-deception. Merely because we hold positions of power we begin to justify and rationalize our decisions. Many times when business power is abused, it is because the powerful have deceived themselves.

Sources of Power

In business many kinds of power operate simultaneously. We will look briefly at a few of these as an introduction to a discussion of the ways Christians should approach power.

Most people view business as a hierarchical structure with defined roles. A certain amount of power comes with each role. Most corporations have a board of directors responsible for the hiring, retention, and oversight of top management, who in turn are responsible for the structure and operation of the business. It is a top-down legal structure with greater authority residing at the highest levels of the organization. Because of this pyramidic structure, the power entrusted to people grows as they ascend the organizational ladder. The impact of their decisions on people and the organization is increased as they are assigned more responsibility.

The kind of power described above, often called positional power, is attached to position. For example, at a college an academic dean has certain power simply because of holding that position. Such authority is a natural result of our efforts to pinpoint authority and responsibility. It is not wrong for some positions to have more decision-making authority than others.

Charismatic power grows from the personal characteristics of people. Some people have almost a mystical quality to influence others with the sheer power of their personality; others have a special ability to persuade with their logic or persuasive arguments.

Power also comes from access to information. People who need information depend on those who have it. One particularly valuable kind of information is knowledge about where and how decisions are made. People also gain power because of their special skills or expert knowledge.

What you know is important, but whom you know can also be a source of power. That is why people often engage in name dropping to gain power. Knowing the right people can give us access to places, positions, and resources that would not be available otherwise.

People in business also control valued and needed resources. The ability to set salaries or determine who is hired for a job or who gets a promotion is power.

The exercise of different kinds of power carries different degrees of coercion. Coercive power limits the choices of the person being influenced or makes any choice but the one the powerful person wants very expensive. For example, it is possible for a victim facing a robber with a loaded gun to refuse to give money, but only at a real risk to health and even life itself. That is coercive power.

Christians will tend to use the kinds of power that give others realistic options. They will avoid coercion, which tries to limit options for other persons. The crucial difference is the amount of real choice that the other person has. This is particularly difficult when working with people who are vulnerable—people who really need a job, or who have invested much of their life in an organization, or older people near retirement, or people whose identity is wrapped up in their job. All of these people have limited power. In difficult situations where decisions need to be made that hurt others, we should always try to work in ways that provide meaningful alternatives, not take advantage of the vulnerability of others.

The Use of Power

We began with the assumption that the use of power is not only necessary but essential for people in business, even Christians. The important question, then, is not whether we will use power, but how.

Our worldview will determine how we define the purpose of power in business. Most managers use power to exercise control. They assign tasks, define objectives, set expectations, evaluate outcomes, and distribute rewards. They use persuasion to encourage people to work for the interests of the company. They allocate resources, make appointments, authorize activities, and make decisions. These are the normal uses of power in an organization.

All managers do these things. Christians try particularly hard to exercise power by using it to serve rather than to dominate. The following list suggests guidelines for all leaders, particularly Christian ones, in their use of power.

1. Good leaders are good followers who work under accountability to others so that they know how to lead and use power.
2. When given responsibility and power, leaders take it and use it. They are courageous and bold, yet humble. They do not run from responsibility with a false sense of humility.
3. They are candid about the power they do have. Powerful leaders who deny that they have power or who do not recognize the power they have are dangerous.
4. Leaders are always concerned about the people in their organizations who do not have power. They look out for them and try to help them gain power.

5. They try to build organizational structures that are characterized by openness and trust. They make decisions through debate and rationality rather than through manipulation, secretiveness, and political maneuvering.

6. They try to open the secrets of the organization and help people learn how to work within it so that people can participate in decisions when they are affected.

7. Good leaders who have power view power as a function, not a status. They know that power is a tool to be used to accomplish goals. Having power does not make a person more important or worth more, or more deserving of special favors than other persons.

We have emphasized the importance of using power to serve. Yet the appropriate use of power can also include directing and giving orders as well as serving. We should willingly take the responsibility to give directions—deciding standards for cleanliness or firing people because of unacceptable behavior. We take the responsibility to make decisions and to take initiative. But we do so in order to serve the purposes of the organization, not to increase our power base or status.

God in Christ gives us a perfect model of a servant leader and the servant use of power. He took a whip to drive the money changers from the temple. But he also washed his disciples' feet to show them that even the Lord of the universe came to serve. He modeled for them how he wanted them to grow as his followers and as leaders in his church. He is our perfect model of a servant leader using power to assist, encourage, and build up followers in stewardship responsibilities.

The Power of Self-Control

The toughest management job any of us face in business, and in all of life, is the job of controlling our own selves. We are called to bring our spirits, intellects, wills, and emotions under the control of Christ. Solomon said it graphically: "Like a city that is broken into and without walls is a man who has no control over his spirit" (Proverbs 25:28). Perhaps better is ". . . he who rules his spirit than he who captures a city" (Proverbs 16:32 NASB).

Self-control is at the core of responsible use of power in business. Self-control is one of the fruits of the spirit (Galatians 5:23). It is Christ's love that must control us and set us free from self-will so we can pursue Christ's will (2 Corinthians 5:14).

In *Leaders* Warren Bennis and Bert Nanus say that leaders must learn to manage themselves. They interviewed ninety leaders, all of whom stressed the importance of self-knowledge. These leaders knew their own abilities and their limits. They were able to admit their mistakes and to learn from them. They became competent in dealing with value conflicts. They did not need to accumulate power themselves to realize their contributions to the organization. Because of that, they were able to work in ways that empowered others. Our ability to use power in a business position is proportional to our ability to control and manage our own lives.

Leaders and managers must also control their personal conduct. If a public leader or corporate executive is unable to manage his or her own private life, others will not trust that person with power or authority in an organization. If we do not keep our private promises, why should people believe that we will keep the public ones? There is little hope of making or adhering to sound corporate policy if our spirit is not under control or if we are guided by selfish pride (Matthew 24:45–47). There is a strong relationship between personal behavior and integrity and public trust.

God realized the need for checks on our self-control. In the Old Testament the power of the Israelite kings was often checked by the power of the prophets. In the New Testament church, ruling was done by a group of elders, not one individual.

Similarly, God expects us to set up checks and balances on our own business power. Self-control works best when we are accountable to superiors and subordinates on a regular basis. Some organizations have subordinates evaluate managers annually. Such checks help managers control their use of power.

QUESTIONS FOR REFLECTION

How Would Jesus Respond to This?

1. Is this picture of business life as a power game an accurate reflection of business life in a sinful society?
2. Discuss whether Christians should view power as a fixed quantity to be divided among the business players. Will one person's increasing power decrease another individual's power? If it will, should Christians concern themselves with it?

Exploring the Bible

1. Read 1 Kings 21:1–28. In what ways do Ahab and Jezebel illustrate the self deception that frequently accompanies power? How does God respond to their abuse of power?
2. Read James 4:1–2 and 7–10. What are the roots of self-control? How can we control our internal power which seeks external expression?
3. Read Matthew 24:45–51 and 1 Peter 5:1–4. Is positional power delegated to us for purposes of ruling or serving?

Contemporary Comment

1. List some settings in which you have felt personally powerful: for example, in your family, your school, your church, your workplace. Examine how you obtained power and whether you used it in a Christian way.
2. The authors suggest that the purpose of power is not control but rather setting God's creation and people free for constructively using resources. Distinguish freedom and control over natural resources from freedom and control over human resources. In which cases do we emphasize freedom? In which control?

3. React to the quote below:

   "When a manager issues the directive or makes the request, he or she is attempting to exercise power. The power is only realized when the other person responds as desired—that is, when he or she 'accepts' the directive or request. Acceptance therefore establishes the limits to power." (John R. Schermerhorn, Jr.)[2]

   Should a Christian manager try to influence his subordinate's level of acceptance?

4. If business power can be easily abused, what types of checks and balances should there be on a manager's decisions?

NOTES

1. From Michael Korda, *Power!* (New York: Random House, 1975), 3–4.
2. John R. Schermerhorn, Jr., *Management for Productivity*, 2d ed. (New York: John Wiley & Sons, 1986), 280.

Chapter 13

ACCOUNTABILITY: STIMULUS FOR SELF-CONTROL

POINT FOR DISCUSSION

A Greenhorn Considers Accountability

At age twenty-two I graduated from college and went to work with my dad. Dad had just bought a plumbing supplies subsidiary sixty miles from the main office. My job was to expand our distribution network and manage the seven employees in the warehouse. I'd been there three months. It was going pretty well. At least I thought so until I overheard Bob, a warehouse employee, during a coffee conversation:

"Yeah, sure, he's a nice kid. He does his job. But him, evaluating me? You've got to be kidding. I've been in this business ten years. I know the job. I know the merchandise. Why he thinks we need a 'special' evaluation session is beyond me."

Bob was right. He did know his job, as did all the other employees. Maybe beginning performance reviews was just an idealistic notion of a college kid. But I worried that Bob's beer-and-football Sundays were getting out of hand. He'd been late a couple of Monday mornings, although he worked those evenings to make up the time. The Monday shipments for which Bob was responsible still went out on time.

Was it my job to comment on his lateness? His drinking? His lack of church attendance? His attitude toward me? Or should I let it go? Maybe I was just trying to establish my authority. After all, Bob was getting his work done. Or would lateness affect performance down the road? What would God want me to do? Should I throw out my ideas about accountability?

The Need for Accountability

One of the more popular myths perpetrated by western secularism is that autonomous people should be held in higher esteem than dependent or interdependent people. Our culture highly values freedom, independence, and self-governance.

Many TV folk heroes are loners who operate outside the rules of society, accountable to no one. Most private eyes of TV fame solve their cases by using techniques that are not really legal. They don't take advice from anybody. Business has its own jungle fighters, self-made men and women who take on the world by themselves. Even religion has its individualistic heroes who stand powerfully on top of a pyramid. These heroes shape our understandings and values in very powerful ways. They honor our society's value of rugged individualism.

Robert Bellah, in *Habits of the Heart*, suggests that the rugged individualism that in the past gave America strength now threatens the survival of freedom itself. A culture in which everyone lives independently, for themselves, cannot last long. Many other social critics feel our failure to recognize our interdependence with others jeopardizes the future of our society.

But there is an even greater reason to raise questions about this way of thinking: it is not biblical.

At the core of individualism is lack of accountability. The Bible, in contrast, calls us to be accountable to God and to other people.

We are called not to be rugged individualists, but members of community. We are to live in relationship to others. One important aspect of this relationship is accountability. One of the reasons Jim and Tammy Bakker got into difficulty is that they were not accountable to a responsible group of advisers or board of directors in a meaningful way. The board they did have was not objective and independent. Nor did Jim and Tammy give them enough information to make careful decisions.

God intends accountability to be a freeing process because it gives direction, security, and encouragement. Imagine a college class where there is no accountability. We would never know if we are doing the right things, nor would we know if we are doing things the way they are supposed to be done. The same is true in business.

Relationships of accountability also provide structures for correction or punishment so that improvement, restoration, and healing might ultimately take place. Accountability was never intended as an end in itself to simply reduce freedom or to create punitive consequences. It is always oriented toward growth and improvement. Our need to be accountable is an acknowledgment of our need for an independent review of our actions and decisions. We need this review to grow and mature.

It is unloving and unfair to give people authority and responsibility but not to hold them accountable for its use or provide the coaching needed to do a good job. There are too many possibilities for misuse of that authority. In organizational structures supervisors are given the responsibility and authority to evaluate those who report to them. We are also informally accountable to our peers and to our subordinates, whose experience and expertise helps us evaluate our conduct more carefully.

In a very real sense our accountability to God is a model for systems of accountability in business. Of course the boss in a business relationship isn't God, even though some bosses act like they are. The boss's responsibilities are far more narrowly defined. Our accountability to God is a relationship with the ultimate purpose of helping us grow and develop. It sets standards for conduct, and gives us the security of knowing when we are doing well. In this sense accountability is a principle that affects all of life, including business. Accountability and the growth of character it creates will better equip us to live authentic Christian lives in the secular marketplace.

The Process of Accountability

Developing a system of accountability when one is new to the group, or with employees who are unaccustomed to it, is a sensitive task, as the Point for Discussion illustrates. The process of accountability places obligations on those who administer the process as well as those who are subject to it. Managers and supervisors who oversee the process are responsible for the establishment of fair standards and regular procedures that guide the report and evaluation process.

The difficulty is in deciding what is fair and on what standards to base evaluation. Is it fair for a manager to inquire about heavy drinking off the job? Is it fair to demand on-the-dot punctuality even when the work is getting done?

Standards that are too low breed poor work habits and encourage people to perform below their ability. Standards that are too high can create frustration and undermine employee self-confidence.

Determining what is a fair standard is not easy. Sarah is a custodian. For many years she has been responsible for cleaning one building. A new supervisor was hired. She evaluated work assignments and concluded that Sarah should be able to clean two floors of another building. Sarah disagreed. How could they determine what was a fair standard? They tried several approaches. First of all they consulted other workers and compared the work Sarah was doing with the others. Then they consulted several other businesses in town to see how they determined a fair workload. They also consulted a national custodial firm to see how many square feet of cleaning they assigned to one worker. They found industry-wide standards published by an industry association. By evaluating all of this information and comparing it to Sarah's experience, they tried to arrive at a fair standard.

After fair standards are determined they must be communicated clearly. All employees, warehouse shippers, machinists, salespeople, secretaries, and managers need to know exactly what is expected. Not only must specific expectations be communicated; the reasons for them and the method of establishing them should be understood by everyone involved.

When people are unaware of a standard, or of a company policy, or of the expectations of their supervisor, they should not be evaluated by that standard. It is not fair to evaluate them as if they had full knowledge of the specific standards.

Effective evaluations should be frequent and follow quickly on the heels of actions. It would not be appropriate for the greenhorn manager in the Point for Discussion to stuff his notes on this issue into Bob's file and wait for a year until his formal evaluation system is running smoothly. In the short run it may seem easier to ignore the problem, but it will usually be more difficult to deal with later. Ignoring or delaying accountability does not help the person involved to grow.

Those who supervise others must also report to a person who supervises them. They must also be responsive to the ideas and feedback on their performance from those they supervise. Paul addresses this need for mutual accountability in Ephesians 5:21: "Submit to one another out of reverence for Christ." The greenhorn manager needs to establish a relationship of mutual accountability with Bob. He must frequently ask for suggestions from the persons he supervises.

Freedom, Control, and Accountability

One criticism often leveled against the principle of accountability is that it reduces freedom and stifles individual creativity. A silly story you probably heard as a child illustrates this point. A little engine pulling four cars got tired and frustrated having to stay on the train tracks. After many miles of complaining, it jumped the tracks and started across the fields on what it thought was a short cut to the next city. It enjoyed the freedom from the constraints of the tracks. But after a few yards it nearly turned over trying to hop over a stump in the pasture. And then only a few yards farther on it got completely stuck in the mud beside a stream.

The little train found that it was most free when it accepted the confines of the track.

Any cooperative effort must include procedures, policies, evaluations, and audits in order for goals to be pursued and accomplished. There must be structure and limits so individual efforts fit together toward a common goal. Imagine how difficult it would be to work on an assembly line if everyone came and went as they chose. Or how frustrated students would become if there were no controls to guide faculty members in their class supervision and grading.

The best kinds of controls are the ones people choose because they see benefit in doing so. In a free society business is a voluntary association of people who choose to work where they do. People generally agree to work at a particular business because they believe that business will satisfy many of their needs.

Employees' needs at work are multiple and complex. Income is an obvious need, but by no means the only one. People want to use their skills in meaningful ways. Social needs are met at work through interaction with other employees. Some want travel opportunities. Others seek a place to be creative. In an effort to satisfy personal needs, people will accept reasonable constraints on their freedom if they can see how these constraints relate to their own objectives and to the larger objectives of the organization.

All of us feel the tension of determining the bounds of freedom. One company may require production workers to wear steel-toed shoes, while another forbids receptionists to chew gum. Businesses also have an obligation to set operating limits which serve customers well.

Limits on ethical freedom are an even tougher area in which to gain business consensus. While Christians should begin with the

Ten Commandments, others may claim greater freedom and act accordingly in business. They may mistakenly assume that more freedom, in moral matters, is automatically better.

Having the ability to choose does not mean we should always have the freedom to choose on issues within the business context. It is reasonable for Christian managers to ask employees to wear protective shoes or limit gum-chewing to break times. It is also appropriate for Christian managers to impose their moral standards via ethical guidelines and audits. While we may prefer self-control and individual freedom at work, policies, procedures, evaluations, and audits are necessary to insure the collective business welfare.

Rewards and Punishments

Sometimes the mere existence of policies and limits is enough to encourage good performance. Occasionally, however, disciplinary systems that include the threat of punishments are necessary. This is particularly true in situations that are not governed by love (1 John 4:18).

Fear of punishment as a continuous emotional condition is certainly negative and not compatible with love and good health. No one should live in a constant state of terror at work. Yet fear, properly understood, can be a positive force in the workplace. People must know for what they are accountable. They must also know the consequences of not living up to that accountability. Even good students are encouraged to study harder for a test because of the fear of receiving an F.

The possibility of negative consequences that have sufficient force to engender fear is a dimension of reality. While love is a more powerful force and a vastly better force for serving people at work, fear is not out of place. Fear will stop some people from acting inappropriately.

A supervisor should never correct, criticize, or penalize an employee without ultimately hoping to build up that person. Any objective short of this goal is unloving and likely to be counterproductive. It is vital for those who administer systems of accountability to provide affirmation in the process of constructively disciplining employees.

Discipline is an aspect of love. The Bible suggests this when it says, "All discipline for the moment seems not to be joyful, but sorrowful; yet to those who have been trained by it, afterwards it yields the peaceful fruit of righteousness" (Hebrews 12:11 NASB). Scripture says plainly that God rigorously disciplines all children of God in love (Hebrews 12:5–13). Discipline and the accompanying fear of it are intended, in God's plan, to be loving dimensions of life and critical parts of any system of accountability.

Failure and Accountability

Failures are a part of life. A critical aspect of development is learning to deal with failure in constructive ways. An important part of supervising others is learning to understand why failures occur and working in ways to help employees grow.

Failures are unquestionably painful. Examples of painful failures include: failing to pass a screening test for a job opportunity, failing to meet a work deadline, or making an error that costs the company a major contract, dealing with a situation in which a coworker gets a promotion to a position we wanted, or failure to get an order that our company really needs. Failures affect us personally. They generate feelings of inadequacy and often cause us to question our worth.

It is important to learn to work with failures so they become opportunities for growth rather than for defeat. It is important to quickly recognize and admit when things are not going well. This allows us to ask for help which can avert a potential failure. Persons who are too proud to admit when things are not going well often continue to drift deeper and deeper into trouble. A failure can point to an area that needs further training. This can be gotten by attending a seminar or arranging for help from a supervisor.

It is also important for us to develop understanding of our own weak and strong areas. This allows us to work in areas in which we are competent. A good supervisor can be very helpful in helping us assess our strengths and weaknesses.

When we have management or supervisory responsibilities we have opportunities to help employees avoid situations which lead to failure. Those responsible for overseeing promotions need to be careful that they do not promote people into situations for which they are not qualified.

Scripture warns those responsible for raising people to positions of authority in the church to make sure those elevated have first been tested (1 Timothy 3:10). The children of God are not put on the fast track. Tested people—people who have faced adversity and overcome it—are excellent candidates for additional responsibility. Occasional crises confront everyone. Those who have weathered them well are good bets to handle the next set of work problems even better.

People may not be able to perform up to expectations for any number of reasons. It is important for supervisors to identify these. Sometimes we must help people accept responsibility for failures that are within their control. If failure is an entrenched pattern, dramatic action or carefully designed programs for improvement may be required. But often there are impediments over which the employee has no control. For example, a printing press operator may be behind schedule because her press is old and breaks down frequently.

Sometimes employees do not know what is to be done or how to do it. Careful job descriptions and training programs remedy these problems.

There are also times when a staff member may feel penalized or punished for good performance. One bricklayer was a particularly good worker and frequently laid more bricks than the other employees. They were paid on a piece rate, so the high performer occasionally got higher wages than his boss, who was paid a salary because he organized and managed jobs. The owner of the company felt the good performer was making too much money, so he lowered the piece rate. This made his coworkers angry. His good performance was rewarded by a penalty. There are many subtle ways this can happen. Sometimes when students do very well on a test the next test is harder or the curve is lowered. Coworkers often get jealous of good performers and use social pressure to get them to slow down. Managers need to be sure that employees are not penalized for good performance.

Another impediment to good performance is present when employees see no reward for doing good work. For example, if the same pay raises are given to poor workers as are given to good ones, there will be little incentive for superior performance.

The key to working at improving performance and dealing with failure is a formal system of performance appraisal and supervision. For Christian managers in business those procedures become very practical ways to implement love and concern for employees.

QUESTIONS FOR REFLECTION

Greenhorn Considers Accountability

1. Should this new college graduate try to *control* these employees? Should he drop his ideas about a performance appraisal system?
2. Will requiring punctuality unnecessarily limit the freedom of employees?

Exploring the Bible

1. Read 2 Chronicles 34:1–2, 14–22. By what means are Josiah and Israel called to accountability? Did this accounting change their behavior? Did this accounting impinge on their freedom? What kinds of standards do Christians have today?
2. Read Romans 14:7–13. Is there a difference between accountability and passing judgment? Explore whether there are ways to emphasize accountability without passing judgment on employees.

3. Read 2 Corinthians 13:1–10. In this example of Christian accountability, what is Paul's goal for the Corinthians? What processes does he use to fairly evaluate their behavior?

Contemporary Comment

1. Do job descriptions, performance appraisal systems, quality inspections, and devices such as time cards achieve the goal of encouraging and enabling people at work? Why or why not?

2. The authors write that it is essential that those who exercise authority over other people place themselves in a system of accountability. To whom should the manager be accountable? Should managers be accountable to their subordinates? To their peers? To their bosses? To their churches? Why should accountability be a two-way street?

3. If people become fearful when they fail to perform well, how should Christian managers react to such fear?

Chapter 14

MOTIVATION: CALLING OR MANIPULATION?

POINT FOR DISCUSSION

Motives and Results

The movie *Wall Street* examines the motives of deal makers involved in sophisticated business finance. Its main character, Gordon Gekko, spends endless work hours on the phone, closing multimillion-dollar deals. On his rare day off Gekko races his ATV past his luxurious beachfront home at top speed against competitors. The same risky, reckless behavior characterizes him at work. He savors the challenge, the speed, and the competitive excitement of beating the stock market and managing a hostile takeover. He believes in himself and the money he makes.

Bud Fox, a rookie stockbroker bored with endless rounds of cold calling, aspires to joining Gekko's inner circle of financial intrigue. He uses inside information on Bluestar Airlines to worm his way into the club. Once inside the operation, however, Bud questions the drives of these incessant workaholics and doubts his own assignment—to secretly track Gekko's chief rival. Bud begins to wonder about motivation, both theirs and his, but has little moral basis on which to evaluate what drives all of them.

Gary Ginter is a real commodities trader, working at the Chicago Board of Trade. He handles thousands of dollars every day in his financial transactions. Gary is a sharp student of the markets, analytical and decisive. He has made a lot of money trading his own account. Yet Gary Ginter lives in a very modest home on the west side of Chicago. Much of the money he makes is channeled directly into a program to finance persons who go to many countries as missionaries supporting themselves through business. Outside of working hours Gary helps his neighborhood in urban redevelopment efforts. Gary Ginter is motivated by his Christian faith.

Motivation

Why do people do what they do? For decades social scientists have been searching for the key that will unlock the secrets of human motivation and answer that question. There are many reasons people want to know the answer; some are good, some not so good. Employers want to know how to get employees to work harder and smarter. Advertisers want to find the secret key that will make people buy their product. Politicians try to find the words or actions that will earn votes. Professors try to motivate students to study. Students try to motivate their professors to give high grades.

We must understand motivation from a moral perspective, both to understand ourselves and to understand how we work with others. We must examine the reasons and forces that influence what we do. We also need to understand what motivates others, since so much of business depends on responding to and influencing other people.

Motivational theorists have been working for years to understand what motivates people in the workplace. All of them seem to agree that we have needs, and that motivation is somehow related to our attempts to meet those needs. But they do not agree on how any one person will try to meet those needs. Some motivational theorists believe actions grow from our need for power, status, wealth, self-esteem, or idealized self-concepts; we may satisfy physiological, psychological, or self-interest needs. Abraham Maslow hypothesized that there is a hierarchy of needs. He suggested that lower-level needs, such as physiological and safety needs, must be met before people can be motivated by higher-level needs, such as the need for belonging, self-esteem, and self-fulfillment. Frederick Herzberg, another motivational theorist, built on this approach by distinguishing between "dissatisfiers" and "satisfiers." "Dissatisfiers," such as salary or supervision, can cause dissatisfaction if they are not adequate; but only "satisfiers," such as responsibility and opportunities for advancement, motivate people to better performance. Herzberg's satisfiers, which motivate people, are at the upper levels of Maslow's hierarchy.

Historically there have been different approaches to motivational theory. We will briefly describe four of these: Freudian, deterministic, cognitive, inheritance.

Freudian theories believe motivation begins with compelling inner drives such as sex and aggression which cause behaviors that will satisfy them. Such drives can be based on prior experience, the modeling of others, or even genetics; but they are always unconscious forces buried deep inside us which control our behavior. This theory would suggest that Gordon Gekko was driven to compete in the world of high finance as a channel for his own natural aggression.

Deterministic theories of human nature hold motivation to be largely programmed by prior experiences. They suggest that human behavior is determined by prior events in a chain-like cause-and-effect pattern. Motives and morals are produced by external experiences and are recorded internally for replay. In this worldview human morality is generally viewed as a conditioned perception. Determinists would argue that Gordon Gekko's actions and reactions were a logical outcome of his early experiences as a financial broker. He played hardball because he was programmed to survive the dog-eat-dog world he experienced each day.

Cognitive theories suggest that motivation is learned by observation. Motivated people modeling certain desirable behaviors such as enthusiasm, perseverance, and quality work attract followers who emulate them. Rewards for such behavior reinforce their value and lead people to repeat them. This theory makes motivation a choice. People are free to choose whether to behave in certain desirable ways. Unfortunately they can also learn undesirable patterns from their leaders. Bud Fox, wanting so badly to emulate Gekko, learned to be a risk-taker, but he also learned to be a cheater. He learned to be motivated by the thrill of winning—no matter what he had to do.

A fourth group of theories posits a role for inheritance in determining motivation. Perhaps some people are born with high motivational tendencies and others with low inclinations to do much of anything. These theorists study whether highly motivated parents tend to have children with above average motivational drives. Some theorists think these factors are genetic; others think they are a function of the social environment. There is also discussion of the relationships of motivation and intelligence. These theorists might conclude that Bud Fox would never ultimately be a wheeler-dealer. It wasn't in his genes or his family's union background.

The Bible emphasizes our responsibility to make choices. Scripture does not approach motivational theory exclusively from any of the above perspectives. It does not recognize any of these as the sole or final source of behaviors. It would not excuse the behavior of Bud Fox or Gordon Gekko because their behavior was somehow outside their control. Instead Scripture speaks about the desires of the heart: the core of our intellect, will, and emotions. Scripture contrasts people who are slaves to their old nature with its drives, passions, and desires, with those who are liberated by Christ and can choose behaviors pleasing to God. Through Christ's power we can deliberately choose a different path for our thoughts and actions. Gary Ginter has consciously chosen a different path from the majority of brokers and traders. So can we.

God examines the intentions behind every action (1 Corinthians 4:5). We are responsible for our conduct. Scripture candidly acknowledges the great gulf that so often exists between what we know we ought to do and what we actually do or do not do (Romans 7:14–25). The Apostle Paul even goes so far as to say there is a "principle that evil is present in [us], the one[s] who wish[es] to do good" (Romans 7:21, NASB). Yet that acknowledgment of evil does not absolve us of responsibility for our conduct.

The heart can be influenced by outside forces; but that still does not absolve us of responsibility. Adam and Eve were deceived by an external agent. It was Satan who tempted them to sin, not God. Adam and Eve were enticed by an apparent good—not a true good—to be like God, knowing good and evil (Genesis 3:5). Despite this manipulation by Satan, God held Adam and Eve accountable for the choice they made. They were morally responsible for both the intentions and the resulting behaviors. They could not get away from responsibility by blaming their actions on each other or on the serpent.

Motivational theories, be they Freudian, deterministic, cognitive, or inheritance, help us understand human behavior. But Scripture adds the dimension of the heart, that conscious source of choice not always emphasized in contemporary theory or practice.

When we consider the roots of motivation, we need to ask two questions. First, what is the basis for Christian motivation? Second, what forms of motivation are appropriate for us to use in motivating other people?

Calling

As Christians we should see our motivation for all that we do as a response to a calling from God. That response requires conscious, willful choices to act in accordance with God's will. We should not wait until we "feel" like responding to God's directives, because following God's call is not based on our feelings. We are to understand motivation as a volitional choice to do something because it is understood to be right. This idea is behind James's statement, "Therefore, to one who knows the right thing to do, and does not do it, to him it is sin" (James 4:17, NASB).

The Apostle Paul writes that Christians are first and foremost called to be saints, people in fellowship with a God of high purposes for the creation (1 Corinthians 1:2–9). This is each Christian's vocation. In this context Christians are called to salvation. The outcome of this salvation is a holy, righteous, and just life. This call requires a conscious commitment of the will to strive against the old nature and to put on a new nature in Christ.

Christians are not called to happiness, though happiness may be a by-product of doing justice; nor are we called to be successful or competitive by the world's standards. We should not be trapped by believing that our primary job in life is to find comfort and personal satisfaction. It's all too easy to become obsessed with the drive to be happy, and to be depressed about the meaning of life when we are unhappy. Instead we are called to ". . . work at it with all [our] heart, as working for the Lord . . ." (Colossians 3:23). Our vocation is loyal, faithful service to our Lord, not personal happiness. We often think about switching jobs, changing our family circumstances, or buying more possessions to increase our happiness. We might look at these decisions very differently if we considered our work for the Lord instead.

This call to be saints is to affect all areas of life, including worship, family life, and work. When Martin Luther understood this, he began to break down the artificial distinctions between glorifying God in the sacred and secular realms of activity. All honorable work, paid or unpaid, is part of our calling. The typist, the pastor, the homemaker, or the sales manager can all serve God and glorify God by diligently serving those around them. Work is an important part of Christian vocation.

John Calvin agreed with Martin Luther that the sacred/secular distinction in vocation was false, and then further defined Christian vocation related to paid occupations. He believed that paid occupations could aid the unfolding of God's kingdom by providing basic goods and services needed to sustain a just and orderly society. He did add the caution that Christians choose their jobs carefully. Because of sin, not all jobs contribute to the health of God's kingdom and its vision of love, service, justice, and community. Yet he affirmed daily work as an important part of Christian calling. Following Christ in obedience can be reflected in service to our neighbors. In business these neighbors are customers, suppliers, distributors, subordinates, and superiors.

For those of us who view all of life as Christian vocation there is a special problem. We must find an appropriate balance between the various parts of life. Work, family, and worship are all important. Community service, leisure and time in solitude are, too. There is no easy formula for balancing these.

We must follow God's leading and the advice and counsel of other Christians. It is so easy to get caught up in one area of life that we do not give adequate attention to the others.

The actions and results of Christians obeying God's will in their occupations may not always lead to different results from those of non-Christians. External outcomes may be the same for both, but internal attitudes will differ immensely. Christians and non-Christians in business may both work for decent earnings per share or a solid return on investment; but Christians should be motivated by a desire to serve God's kingdom by serving others, while non-Christians are motivated by self-defined needs or desires. The purposes for Christian actions and decisions will be unique, though the outcomes may be the same; God weighs those differences in purpose carefully.

Doug Sherman's recent article, "Does God Need Pallets?" illustrates the outcomes of a Christian sense of vocation.[1] Pallets are the platforms used in transporting goods to make it easier for forklifts to load and unload stacks of goods. Doug Sherman has a friend who made pallets. How could his pallet-maker friend be doing God's work? How could making pallets possibly fit into God's work in the world? He answered the question by pointing out that pallet makers are an important link—along with truckers, farmers, grocers, box makers, and bankers—in the chain of activity that supplies food for his family. Since meeting the needs of families is God's work, the Christian pallet maker can work with the belief that he is serving God in this world.

We should go into business with the same sense of call, the same need for accountability, and the same willingness to sacrifice for the Kingdom of God as does the minister or full-time church worker.

Manipulation

Exploring personal motivations is only half the picture. The other half is our efforts to influence the motivations of others. Managers are continually trying to motivate employees to produce more or work better as a team. This is necessary and appropriate. However, when motivational techniques are deceptive or when they force people to do things against their will, motivation becomes manipulation.

Most employers and managers have a strong interest in motivational theories and techniques because they wish to modify behavior and improve the bottom line for the business. Supervisors are evaluated by their unit's accomplishments. This reality leads to a strong interest in motivational techniques that bring about effective results. Behavior and results are the watchwords. Intents, motives, and attitudes seem less important in the view of many business professionals unless they can be linked to results.

The emphasis on behavior and results fosters incentive systems, disciplinary processes, training programs, and team management techniques that aim to motivate people to greater efficiency and productivity. This is good because true stewardship requires efficiency and productivity. It is commendable to do a better job of managing the created order. That glorifies God, reveals the wonder of God in creation, and services other people more effectively.

This emphasis on behavior and results can have negative consequences, however, because the very success realized through motivational techniques encourages the belief that employees are only a means to be manipulated in creating wealth. People may be coaxed, channeled, directed in any way possible as long as the results are good for the firm. Even the commonly quoted textbook definition of management—"working *through* people to get things done"—reflects this. Increasing market share, meeting a sales quota, getting deliveries out on time, or reducing material waste are worthy objectives. Yet there are limitations on the motivational techniques used to reach these objectives.

God endowed each of us with a will. When motivational techniques are used deceptively or to undermine a person's conscious choices they are abusive. People are more than means of production.

Three criteria can help us handle motivational tools appropriately:

1. *Those who motivate others must appeal to good motives.* Suppose a company motivated sales representatives by promises of a company-paid wild week for two at a Caribbean motel named "Hedonism." No questions would be raised about who participates or their behavior. This type of reward motivates employees to work because they dream about spending their time in unwholesome activities. Appealing to such drives does not expand Christian values in society. Instead a company could encourage sales personnel with promises of a "relaxing resort vacation with your spouse."

   Some automobile dealers appeal to buyers on the basis that a car conveys upper-class status. To do so motivates them to differentiate themselves in society on the basis of what they own. Might Christian dealers appeal to function, safety, and fuel efficiency as well as styling? It would lessen status as a motivating force.

   Lotteries in many states tap the desire to get rich quick without work. In the long term these values, promoted over and over again on television, radio, and newspapers, could have destructive effects on North American society.

Christians should appeal to motives that will benefit society in the long term and which are in harmony with the will of God. We can appeal to the celebration of employee talents, family togetherness, or community service. McDonalds's ads portray such values regularly. AT&T encourages us to "reach out and touch someone." We can appeal to healthy motives if we try.

2. *Christians must be open and honest about the motivational techniques they are using.* Subtle forms of motivation are manipulative because the people being influenced are not aware of what is happening. These techniques are wrong because they are dishonest.

A need for open explanations of the reasons behind motivational techniques becomes more critical with complex motivating systems. Employees should understand what behaviors the company bonus formula is encouraging. They should be educated about the effects of sensitivity training on group relationships. They should be told about the goals for techniques such as quality circles.

To use motivating devices without explanation treats people as objects. It assumes that they do not need to know how the systems and procedures of a company shape their behavior. People deserve to understand the forces that affect them.

3. *Healthy motivational approaches encourage active choices on the part of participants.* They help identify alternatives and options and the costs and opportunities in each choice. They also facilitate growth in decision making. Manipulation controls outcomes so tightly that those affected have little choice but to comply. Part of what it means to be "made in the image of God" is to be able to make choices that really make a difference. Assembly workers with power to stop their line when the output is defective are in a much healthier motivational climate than workers whose only job is to comply with a specified rate of five parts per minute.

We should not use motivational techniques that manipulate because they often appeal to motives which are wrong, they are often dishonest, and they do not give people meaningful choices.

Christians as Motivators

Christians do have a contribution to make in the development of theories of motivation. We should develop as complete an understanding of human motivation as possible because human motivation is tied directly to human need. Our role in life is to follow Christ, who in turn calls us to serve each other. We serve in part by helping people both recognize their true needs and then satisfy those needs in healthy and creative ways. Servants must know the needs of those they would serve.

New research is currently expanding our understanding about the wide range of variables that affect motivation. While theorists of the past offer helpful insights into the roots of human behavior and the role of rewards and punishments, new findings focus on motivating employees through participatory decision making, team work, better human resource policies, and a shared company vision. These fresh approaches offer fruitful ground for Christian managers. They are built on notions of responsibility and community which seem more compatible with Christian views of calling. They treat people as more than means of production.

We should feel responsible for removing obstacles to healthy motivation. If employees are eager to learn, to perform, and to expand their knowledge, Christian employers should help. It is our job to develop the skills and talents of people. Motivation shackled by a lack of praise, ill-defined job descriptions, or a lack of information about company goals, thwarts growth. Sometimes the best motivational technique is clearing the underbrush so the paths to service and achievement can be seen.

Finally, the significant difference between a Christian and secular view of motivational techniques is one of attitudes, intent, and results. The heart is the conscious root of human character and behavior. Intentions are important, but so are results. God will judge both motives and outcomes. The rightness of anything is inseparably connected to its sources as well as to its outcome. When human sincerity, constancy, and love are absent or artificial, the motivational relationship will eventually suffer.

QUESTIONS FOR REFLECTION

Motives and Results

1. Discuss contemporary movies and books that describe business motives. How do you react to them as a Christian?
2. What do you think motivates Gary Ginter? Would you feel comfortable as a Christian in his job?

Exploring the Bible

1. Read Psalm 40:1-8. What should be the Christian's source of motivation?
2. Read Luke 12:15-31. What made it wrong for the rich man to plan for bigger storage barns?
3. Read Romans 7:14-25. What effect does the law of sin have on our motivations and the motivations of those with whom we work? Does the law of sin explain why we sometimes purposely do things we know are wrong?

Contemporary Comment

1. Evaluate your own sense of calling. In what ways are you answering God's call for you by studying business?
2. Should we discard the use of specific motivational tools such as piecework pay and sales bonuses because they could be manipulative?
3. Is there any value or any danger in describing people at work as "human resources" or "human assets"? Should we describe them with the same types of names we use for natural resources or financial assets?

4. Suppose Joe, depressed, comes into your office upset about his wife's constant nagging and threats of divorce. Joe could stay all afternoon explaining his problem and his feelings. However, as his manager you are responsible for being sure Joe gets some work accomplished, for helping other workers with some inventory problems, and for returning some calls to key customers. What decisions do you make about time that afternoon? If you send Joe back to immediate tasks to be done, are you treating him as a means of production?

NOTES

1. Doug Sherman and William Hendricks, "Does God Need Pallets?" from *Your Work Matters to God* (Colorado Springs, CO: New Press, 1987).

Chapter 15

COMMUNICATION: LISTENING AND TRUTH-TELLING

Something to Hide?

"I got called into my boss's office on Monday and got [chewed out] up and down and left and right about a Bible study I have been leading. My boss said to me, 'I want you to answer one question. Have you been having a Bible study in your office from 4:00 to 5:00 on Monday afternoons?' And I said, 'Yes.'

She said, 'That is totally inappropriate, and I will not allow you to do that anymore, I'm very upset with you.' Laurie explained that she finished her duties at 3:30, that no one was participating in the Bible study during a scheduled period of work, and that no one was proselytizing in the hospital. Her explanation did not resolve the conflict. "I got up and said, 'If that's what you want' and walked back to my office—and cried and cried. I said, 'Oh, Lord, what do you want me to do about this?'"

Laurie realized that she had put her supervisor in an awkward position and that the supervisor had probably been reprimanded by the director of nursing. "I realized that I had been a coward last April when we started this study. I knew then I probably should tell her, but I did not want to because I thought she would say 'no.' So I rationalized and thought, 'It's over and above work time, and it's none of her business. It's in my office, and we're not hurting anybody.' But I knew. I knew all along that sooner or later it would be found out and I would really be in big trouble. I thought about it and concluded, 'Laurie, it's not fair. You put her in a really bad situation, and you must go and apologize.' "

The supervisor could be stern, and the last thing Laurie wanted to do was reopen the conflict, but she knew what God was calling her to do. She left a note on her supervisor's desk, asking her to page her when she had time. "She paged me, and I went down to her office. Once I get started, I'm extremely direct. I said, 'I called this meeting because I want to apologize to you. I am sorry you had to be surprised with something that I should have come to you about directly, rather than your having to hear it from someone else.' She just nodded her head, and there was a firm line about her mouth. I said, 'I will not do this again. I'm sorry.' She said, 'Well, as far as I'm concerned, if you want to meet, you may meet in the chapel, but you have to go through the proper channels.' Then things were fine. Our work relationship was back to where it had been, and I was pleased . . ."[1]

The Need for Careful Communication

"People are not mind readers." That's obvious, isn't it? Not really. Peter Drucker, an internationally known management consultant, uses this statement in a management training film to emphasize the importance of clear and open communication in business. Think how often you assumed that others should understand your actions without your telling them why you did what you did. Or how often you assumed you knew what another person thought without asking directly.

In the Point for Discussion Laurie's failure to communicate created a difficult situation. She resolved that situation by open and clear communication. We communicate all the time by our behavior and speech; but we cannot always be sure that what we think we are saying is what people are hearing. We normally have a good idea what it is we want to say, but there is less certainty what others perceive. There are often significant gaps between our intentions and others' perceptions. Speaking clearly is important, but listening carefully is even more significant.

The New Testament describes listening as the cornerstone of good communication. We often have a hard time really hearing what other people are saying. The Apostle James tells us we should be quick to hear and slow to speak (James 1:19). Christ also understood our hearing problem: "He who has ears, let him hear" (Matthew 11:15; 13:9, 43). His listeners heard the words, but didn't put them into action.

Successful communication demands that we tailor our message to fit the nature and capacity of the listeners. King Solomon put it this way: "The tongue of the wise makes knowledge acceptable" (Proverbs 15:2 NASB). Good communicators adopt language and illustrations that listeners will be able to understand. Communicating for understanding is hard work.

Robert E. Lee, the famous Civil War general, was noted for his diligent efforts to communicate in ways that his listeners understood. He never sent a communiqué to one of his generals before first asking a private to read the message. Then the private had to state in his own words what action was being requested. If he could not respond with the message Lee intended, Lee assumed the fault was his own lack of clarity, not the private's. He would then rewrite the message as many times as necessary to clarify it.

Good communicators learn to listen even while they are talking. They learn to "read" their audience. They can identify the signals that say their audience is no longer paying attention. Facial expressions can indicate confusion and puzzlement. People communicate with their body language the entire time someone else is speaking. It is almost impossible to maintain a "poker face," a conscious effort not to communicate through eyes, facial expressions, nervous fidgeting, or body posture.

Once we have spoken we must also listen carefully to the feedback we receive from others. Robert H. Waterman, Jr., in his book *The Renewal Factor*, describes managers who constantly adjust and renew qualities in their organizations that keep them growing and on the cutting edge. In one chapter, entitled "A Different Mirror," he stresses the need for managers to be good listeners. They constantly listen for perceptions of their company or ideas of how things can be improved.

Listening Is Costly

The world is full of defensive, opinionated, distracted, ignorant, and otherwise impaired listeners. Why are there so few good listeners in the world? Because it is risky to be an open listener. Closed people who don't listen well are prone to excuse, justify, ignore, or reject truth. They isolate themselves from the feelings and opinions of others. They just don't hear. In the short run this might seem easier than taking the opinions and ideas of others seriously. But it is not best in the long run, nor is it the way Christians are called to act.

Careful listening requires response. Open listeners are willing to be corrected and are not defensive. They acknowledge their need to learn from others. They are very vulnerable and will at times be hurt. Open listeners learn when they are inaccurate, misunderstood, or ignored; they are often challenged to change, grow, and serve. They are constantly humbled as they risk confrontations with truth.

Imagine the following situation in a welding shop. Jeff, a spot welder, says to you, his supervisor, "You claim to care about our working conditions but you don't know what they are. I haven't seen you on the floor of the shop for months." The natural reaction to such an accusation is defensiveness. Most of us would quickly think of excuses that have "necessitated" being off the floor for the past four months. A closed listener begins to formulate excuses because being caught in such an out-of-touch state is very embarrassing. The reasons for the absence come flooding out, communicating to Jeff that his problems are less important than the manager's reasons for absence. Defensive attitudes shut down communication and open the doors to more serious problems later.

An open listener accepts the truth. The conversation might continue, "Jeff, it's true. I have been off the floor for a good while now. What's happening out there? I'd really like to know." The open listener acknowledges his absence and his unfamiliarity with the current situation on the floor of the shop.

Jeff, the accuser, continues: "Joe put this new trainee, Jim, on the machine next to me fourteen weeks ago and it has been all downhill since. Jim just doesn't understand how things should be done. I probably wasn't too tactful, but gee, he let oil get in the aisle by his machine. He parked his finished goods dolly so it interfered with my work, and he interrupts me every other minute for some kind of help. Joe won't help, you aren't around to help, and I am up to my ears with his mistakes."

The opinionated listener would fit Jeff's account of the events into a preconceived interpretation of the situation. He assumes that he knows the real problem behind the events without needing to hear Joe's analysis. He may quickly dismiss Jeff's ideas because Jeff is a "complainer." Or he may be so committed to other tasks that he has no time to pursue the matter.

The open listener, on the other hand, hears the report and takes it seriously. Like Laurie, in the opening Point for Discussion, he realizes that "the first to present his case seems right" (Proverbs 18:17). The manager acknowledges his need to do some more listening. Joe, the foreman, needs to tell his side of the story. The new trainee's situation needs to be evaluated. Our open listener will also own his share of the problem. He has been distracted for fourteen weeks by other pressures and has neglected the shop floor.

Resolution of this situation requires careful listening. It is easy for Jeff to blame Jim, the new trainee, for the situation. Then Jim might blame Joe because of lack of proper orientation. You, the supervisor, might conclude that the new trainee is not very smart or is not trying hard. You might conclude that Jeff is too picky.

One of the keys to resolving this situation is for the supervisor to encourage careful listening among all the people involved. The supervisor needs to hear from each person. The trainee needs to hear how his actions affect Jeff. Jeff needs to hear suggestions of how he might be helpful to the new person. The supervisor needs to hear how he might improve his supervision. A system of open communication where all the people can hear from each other would go a long way to resolve the situation.

This might happen in a number of ways. You might invite the whole group to discuss the situation over coffee. You would try to keep the discussion focused on the problem and to avoid personal accusations. You might help each person understand the problem from the other's point of view by asking each one to put himself in another person's position and explain things from that perspective. When one person makes a statement you might ask another person to repeat that statement to be sure that it is heard and understood. You might invite a person trained in organizational communication to serve as a facilitator for a conversation.

An open listener, whatever the situation, takes seriously what is being said. The direct message is important but so are the feelings and hidden messages behind the stated one.

This kind of listening is costly, and takes a lot of time. There is always the possibility that people will say things we don't want to hear, or things that are unfair or not true. Real listening usually requires that we change—and we all know how hard that is.

The Rewards of Listening

Listening includes being vulnerable to the reactions of others. It also helps us discern their needs, making us better servants and stewards. Jeff, the welder described earlier, had need. As long as that need was not heard it could not be satisfied. It created frustration. But when needs are met employees are free to be constructively creative. For this reason listening is essential to encouraging growth and development of God's people.

The resolution of conflicts in business requires careful listening. Only when we listen can we find opportunities to acknowledge prior misunderstandings or recognize equally valid and acceptable alternatives. We can resolve differences through understanding, which rests on good listening.

Listening to the insights of others is the first step in self-evaluation. The perspectives of other people can be very helpful as we examine ourselves in the light of God's standards to determine our obedience to God's will. "If we judge ourselves rightly, we [will] not be judged" (1 Corinthians 11:31 NASB). If we listen carefully we can judge whether we have been true to God's call.

Listening builds trust. This is necessary if people at work are to be open and honest. Poor listening habits invite and foster dishonest communication. Effective listening invites understanding.

The rewards of listening are enormous. Listening is a basic building block of learning, which helps us mature. Those who truly listen gather facts, opinions, and value statements. These are ingredients of knowledge, understanding, and wisdom. Godly managers ultimately need understanding and wisdom, a gift of God, if they are to be effective stewards and servants. Listening is one of the primary components of wisdom. It has been said that none of us learns very much by hearing ourselves speak.

Misdirected Communication

A second problem in communication is the failure of people who have concerns to discuss them directly with those who are involved. Call it gossip, back-biting, complaining, whatever you will. It's usually just plain sinful undercutting of those who irritate us.

There are many reasons for misdirected communication in business. One reason is our desire to hide our basic insecurity. We may put someone down because we think this will make us look better.

Or we may put a second party in a bad light or shift blame from ourselves to someone else, leaving that person with no opportunity to respond. We may, in fact, have little interest in accuracy, fairness, or reconciliation. Without thinking of the consequences we ventilate our feelings, dumping them on the wrong people, to elevate our own weak identities. It would have been easy for Laurie in the Point for Discussion to do just this by sniping at her supervisor or talking behind her back.

Another common reason for misdirected communications is personal hurt. Some people take responsibility for the hurt on themselves and become depressed. They blame themselves and lower their own self-esteem. Others dump their hurt on uninvolved third parties. They'll tell almost anyone they meet about their hurt, and about the person who inflicted it.

Hurt and its resulting anger often get buried and end up being vented on people who can do little to resolve the problem. While venting feelings provides temporary emotional relief, it does nothing to bring about reconciliation and often hurts others.

Whether we are dealing with our own insecurities or inflicted hurt, both parties should get together to discuss the problem and its causes. This is why God says, "In your anger do not sin. Do not let the sun go down while you are still angry" (Ephesians 4:26). Backbiting, gossip, and tearing others down occur far too frequently at work. God has given us directions for dealing with them.

It is not good to ignore hurts. It is important to find creative and constructive ways to deal with them.

Some people vent their anger through exercise—running, handball, or aerobics. Some kick the dog when they get home or take it out on the family. Others gossip. Some try to undermine their coworkers. Releasing pent-up frustration through vigorous physical exercise is an effective way of venting pent-up anger without harming anyone. It does not help to blow up at the person who hurt us, or the next person we happen to meet. That too often aggravates the problem and causes further alienation.

Matthew 18:15–17 gives a series of steps for resolving situations in which we think we have been wronged by others. The direct meaning of this passage applies to brothers and sisters in the church, but it extends to business as well.

The first step is to discuss the grievance directly with the person who committed the wrong. If it can be resolved in that conversation the Bible says that we will have restored the relationship. That is the goal of talking about the wrong.

If that does not work the Bible suggests taking along one or two other people. They can assist with communication, and they also bring a helpful objectivity. Often third parties like these can think of solutions that the participants in the conflict cannot see. They can help the disagreeing parties to hear each other.

The third step is to report the incident to the authorities. In business this would include supervisors. Again the objective is to use those resources to find a good resolution.

Increasing the ability to properly resolve conflicts and to constructively direct anger is essential if healthy relationships are to prevail in business. It takes hard work and much practice to overcome bad habits; but it's possible to learn better, more biblical patterns. The rewards are many.

Honest and Clear Expression

We are often taught by experience that it is risky to be honest. Honesty is sometimes rewarded by rejection or retaliation. Many of us have been taught by supervisors, executives, parents, or pastors to be so tactful or polite that we often become dishonest. The commonly used expression "honest to a fault" shows that contradiction. How can one find fault with honesty? The expression implies that too much truth is risky because it can hurt us and others.

Employees sometimes find that their supervisors respond better if they tell them what they want to hear rather than the straightforward truth. Politicians would not get elected if they told us the truth about some of the difficult problems the country faces or even about their own policies. Strong leaders frequently employ weak subordinates because they do not want to hear disagreement. They hide behind the facade of agreement because of an insecure personality. Or they may be so full of pride that they cannot accept the ideas of others.

Salespeople often bend the truth in conversations with customers. They may tell the customer what they think the customer wants to hear rather than what is actually correct. It is so easy to slip in false information about competitors to complete a sale, or to feign ignorance about product shortcomings. One Christian appliance salesman would often try to convince a potential customer that he was offering a good deal by saying something like, "Last week I sold four of those refrigerators." The employees knew he had sold none. That may look like a harmless exaggeration, but the employees often discussed among themselves whether or not they could trust anything he said. They could never be sure that he was telling the truth about other things.

In the Sermon on the Mount Jesus said that Christians should not swear oaths because they should always tell the truth. He said, "Simply let your 'Yes' be 'Yes' and your 'No,' 'No' " (Matthew 5:37). We should tell the truth simply, directly, and without pretense.

An incident in the life of Jesus shows that he did this. Philip brought Nathaniel to Jesus. When Philip told Nathaniel about Jesus, Nathaniel asked, "Can any good thing come out of Nazareth?" (John 1:46 NASB). Nathaniel expressed an honest, direct question. Galilee was a poor region separated from Jerusalem and Judaea by Samaria. Nazareth was a layover city on a main trade route north of Jerusalem. Its night life was loose. Nathaniel expressed his honest doubt about whether a leader of Israel could emerge from such an environment.

How did Jesus respond to such honesty? Jesus greeted Nathaniel, "Behold, an Israelite indeed, in whom there is nothing false!" (John 1:47). There was no pretense with Nathaniel. Jesus did not take offense at Nathaniel's blunt question. Instead he welcomed such a direct frank inquiry. That is a model for response to straightforward comments.

The truth, though, must be handled in love if it is to reflect Christ's character (Ephesians 4:15). Truth can be used cruelly, tactlessly, and rudely rather than in constructive and healing ways. In business we should take the need for complete honesty seriously, but we must simultaneously communicate concern for those affected by the message. A regular customer will be disappointed if we suggest that her first choice may not be the best match for her needs. An employee will be depressed when we point to inadequate performance that is hindering promotion. We must respond to these feelings and work with them.

Love is not well served by inaccurate, incomplete, masked, or misdirected communication. Neither are people at work well served when we tell the truth in a brutal, harsh, or condemning manner. There are times we need not say everything we know even though it is true. Listening and then speaking the "truth in love" should characterize our communications.

QUESTIONS FOR REFLECTION

Something to Hide?

1. What should Laurie have done when she started planning the Bible study?
2. Should Laurie have gone back to talk with the supervisor after the reprimand? Would you have been able to do that?

Exploring the Bible

1. Read Proverbs 10:19–21. Why does this wisdom writer suggest that sin and foolishness are linked to a multitude of words?
2. Read James 3:3–12. How powerful is the spoken word? Is it better to listen than to speak?
3. Read Matthew 18:15–17. How should Christians handle communication sins in the workplace? How does the opening vignette for this chapter illustrate one Christian's approach to resolution?

Contemporary Comment

1. What does the quality of our listening say about how we value people?

2. Max DePree says in *Leadership Is An Art* that:

> A number of obligations go along with good communication. We must understand that access to pertinent information is essential to getting a job done. The right to know is basic. Moreover, it is better to err on the side of sharing too much information than risk leaving someone in the dark. Information is power, but it is pointless power if hoarded. Power must be shared for an organization or a relationship to work.
>
> Everyone has a right to, and an obligation for, simplicity and clarity, in communication. We owe each other truth and courtesy, though truth is sometimes a real constraint, and courtesy, inconvenient. But make no mistake—these are the qualities that allow communication to educate and liberate us.[2]

Is information power? If Christians are to empower others, do employees have a right to full information about their organization? How should the right to know be balanced with the need to keep information from competitors and to protect rights of personal privacy?

3. Organizations that desire to communicate with employees openly and honestly must set up communication systems to do so. How can an organization help ensure honest communication at all levels?

NOTES

1. From Patricia Ward and Martha Stout, *Christian Women at Work* (Grand Rapids, MI: Zondervan, 1981), 177–178. Copyright © 1981 by The Zondervan Corporation. Used by permission.
2. Max DePree, *Leadership Is An Art* (New York, NY: Doubleday and Co., Inc., 1989), 98–99.

PART 4

Business: An Agent for Shalom

Chapter 16

THE SOCIAL CONTRACT OF BUSINESS

Our Mission in Business

The mission of God's people is to carry out the total redemptive task of Jesus Christ.

The Great Commission calls us to make disciples of all nations, to baptize and to teach all that Jesus commanded. It calls us to express the totality of his teaching and relationships. As the Father sent him, so he sends us.

Jesus fulfilled the Old Testament vision of shalom, which describes God's intention for creation. Shalom is God's vision of what "ought to be." It is a vision of peace, justice, and salvation. It is a vision of spiritual, physical, and social wholeness and well-being.

How do we conduct business as mission? We extend shalom into our business relationships and there carry out the redemptive activity of Jesus, bearing witness to the transforming gospel in all its dimensions.

As Christians in business our mission is to honor God in the world of work and economics by extending his reign to all our activities. With Jesus as lord of the marketplace, our task is to love, serve, preach, and heal. We use our faith, skills, and resources to correct inequities, work toward economic justice, seek righteousness, bring hope where there is no hope, and make all things new.

Business as mission can take many forms:

- practicing corporate shalom by ensuring that relationships, profits, products, and ethics correspond with God's intention for humanity
- investing in things that affirm and enhance life and refusing to invest in things that harm or diminish life
- doing business in problem areas of the world and there model the kingdom way
- using our economic and political power on behalf of the powerless
- doing business in a way that supports the mission of the church
- evangelization and church planting through business
- carrying out economic development to bring physical and economic wholeness to the needy. [1]

Business: An Agent for Shalom

"Please write on a piece of paper the name of a person in this town who lives a Spirit-filled life." This request was given at the close of a discussion on the Spirit-filled life at a meeting of the ministerial association of a small town in eastern Pennsylvania. Each of the thirteen ministers wrote a name. When the slips were read, every one had named Elmer. Elmer was the owner of a feed mill, not a minister or full time church worker, but a businessman. For him, business provided an opportunity to express commitment to Jesus Christ through his relationships. For him business was mission.

Shalom is a Hebrew word used more than 350 times in the Bible to describe the world as God intended it to be. Today the word shalom has often been reduced to simply mean "peace." But that hardly scratches the surface of its rich meaning in the Bible. To experience shalom is to be whole, sound, and safe; to be healthy and to prosper. It is to be in complete harmony with God, self, others, and the entire created order.

God calls us to be agents of shalom in the world. Can we do that in business? Yes! In fact, Christian businesspeople are to be just that—servants of God who act as stewards in ways that show God's will at work, play, worship, and in the family. Business, as an institution, provides the opportunity to participate with God in the creation and distribution of God's wealth in God's world. Christians are to foster shalom in their place of work.

We promote shalom when we do justice and righteousness, when we love and exemplify kindness and mercy, and when we walk humbly with God. Shalom will not be experienced in its fullness until everyone submits to the Lordship of Jesus Christ; but in the meantime we are to be models and proponents of shalom, everywhere.

Society's Expectations for Business

In recent years there has been a revolution in the way people understand the relationship between business and society. In the past a business that made a profit, provided an acceptable place to work, paid a going wage, and obeyed the law was considered to have done a good job. No more. In the future business will be judged not only for its economic contributions, but for its social, political, and moral ones as well.

Business has responded to these changes in expectations in a number of ways. A lot of effort is placed on making work meaningful and safe. Products are monitored to make sure they are safe. New forms of management encourage employee participation in decision making. Profit-sharing plans and employee-owned businesses are increasing. Business is finding new ways to protect the environment.

Society's emerging view of business, which emphasizes its responsibility to contribute to a good life for all, is in many ways consistent with the Christian view of business as mission. It opens up many opportunities for Christians to live their faith.

The expectations that society has of business and the expectations business has of society are often called a "social contract." This social contract is not written in one place. Parts of it are informal, while other segments have been formalized. It is not even the same in every city or state. Many factors determine its content. There are cultural assumptions—as much free choice as possible, rule by law, and sacredness of life, for example. Common law guides property rights and contracts. Legislation has established regulatory bodies, social security laws, and antitrustlaws. Judicial rulings have established such concepts as the hiring of aggrieved minorities in certain cases.

The social contract is altered by many forces and thus constantly changes. Over the past century changing technology, shifting moral values, and irresponsible business behavior have been particularly influential. For example, legislation dealing with chemical waste was enacted as a direct result of polluting technology. A whole new set of expectations will need to be developed to respond to genetic engineering and other discoveries in biotechnology. Most anti-discrimination legislation reflects shifts in moral consciousness toward the treatment of minorities. "Truth-in-lending" laws, requiring that interest rates be truthfully stated, came into being because rates were not always stated honestly.

One of the key elements of the social contract in our society is the free enterprise system, which is based on competition and freedom of choice. Business must compete for sales and profits. Over the long run we assume that firms that satisfy consumer needs and wants will survive, and those which do not will fail. The private enterprise system provides for a maximum amount of freedom of choice for individuals in employment, purchases, and investments. Companies must continually adjust their strategies to respond to the choices people make.

Adam Smith, often called the father of capitalism, coined the phrase "the invisible hand of competition." This is the process that regulates the choices of individuals in such a way that all the decisions added together serve the common good. He saw capitalism as an efficient means to provide the most goods and services to the most people most of the time.

Capitalism has many strengths. It encourages businesses and individuals to work hard and take the right risks by rewarding them with higher incomes and profits. It also punishes those who take wrong risks. It is efficient at producing goods, and it provides a variety of choices to consumers—consider, for example, the many kinds of toothpaste and soap on a drugstore shelf. It does many things well.

Americans feel comfortable with capitalism and are not inclined to change to other economic systems that would have public ownership of economic production and distribution. Nor are they very willing to give up freedom of choice.

However, our society is changing its expectations of the economic social contract. When the gap in wealth between the rich and poor increases, there are attempts by government and other groups to equalize opportunity and wealth. There is recognition that those at the bottom of the economic ladder are not always well served. Many people feel that society has a responsibility to provide for the special needs of the poor, the physically and mentally disadvantaged, and the chronically unemployed. Legislation in the 1970s and 1980s, such as the Vocational Rehabilitation Act and the Job Partnership Training Act, reflects these concerns.

The Bible says, "The righteous care about justice for the poor, but the wicked have no such concern" (Proverbs 29:7). Just because an economic system does a good job of providing for the physical well-being of most people does not excuse society if it ignores the needs of those who are unjustly treated. Business responsibilities in contemporary society extend beyond satisfying the customer and turning a profit.

Business provides many opportunities for Christians to exercise social responsibility. We can take leadership in working to narrow the gap in income and wealth between the rich and the poor without encouraging dependence or laziness. In New York City a businesswoman is helping poor people begin their own small businesses. In Haiti a group of Christian businesspeople are providing loans and business advice to storefront businesses. In Michigan Christian entrepreneurs are opening retail outlets for the products of Third World cottage industries. Self-help Crafts, in Ephrata, Pennsylvania, markets crafts from all over the world in gift shops throughout the United States and Canada, sending the profits back to the people in developing countries.

Poverty is the result of many factors. The disadvantaged can be suppressed. Individuals and economic groups can take advantage of ignorance or use their favored position to deny equitable opportunities to the less powerful. Minimum wage laws, legislation supporting unions, and antidiscrimination regulations are all efforts to protect people from such exploitation. Some people are poor because they are complacent or do not work. Still other people struggle from disabilities and circumstances that are no fault of their own. We should seek ways to help these people that do not create dependency and do encourage self-help efforts.

The economic system itself also works against certain people. Plant closings or obsolescent skills leave people unemployed. Young people growing up in pockets of poverty often do not learn the social and technical skills needed to succeed. Some people cannot even find the first rung of the economic ladder, let alone climb it!

God judges economic systems that foster blatant misallocation of wealth and do not provide for the welfare of all people. One example of God's interest in economic policy is described in Leviticus 25:8-34. Part of God's contract and covenant with Israel included a fifty-year Jubilee in which all land was to be returned to the original owners. The Jubilee was designed to prevent the financial burdens and mistakes of one generation from being carried on the backs of future generations. Imbalances were not to be perpetuated. Every fifty years the Israelites were given a chance to begin again. In addition, debts were to be canceled every seven years. This provision encouraged lenders to help their borrowers be financially prudent, and encouraged the lenders to be charitable. Like Jubilee, debt cancellation kept borrowers from becoming perpetual slaves of lenders.

Society expects businesses to be partners in alleviating poverty. So does God, who desires a good life for all people, a life free from economic slavery and repression. When we are creative and prayerful we can find strategies that work. Some successful entrepreneurs from a suburban Milwaukee church felt their faith required them to find jobs for unemployed minorities from their inner city. In just a couple of years, with the help of a local black pastor, they have found stable jobs in their companies for over fifteen adults. Some of these people had not worked in years. One twenty-eight-year-old man had never had a job. It's a challenging project, but faith, prayer, and careful planning are dramatically changing the lives of these poor people and their families.

The social contract is broader than taking responsibility for alleviating poverty. It includes interaction with consumers, suppliers, shareholders, the local community, governments, the environment, and a host of other factors. Yet working to alleviate poverty is one important aspect of our Christian responsibility. In that cause Christians should be at the forefront. We should head efforts to make the social contract more just. God expects it as we extend shalom.

What About Profits?

The social contract with business defines the framework of rules within which business operates. It does not stipulate the purpose of individual businesses, nor does it define the purpose and goals of individuals who work in business.

If you ask a businessperson, particularly a business owner, "Why are you in business? What is your purpose?" the most frequent answer is, "To make a profit." How do Christians react to that response? Should the chief end of business be to make money? What is the appropriate role of profit? What are worthy goals for Christians in business? The way we answer these questions will profoundly shape our conduct.

Profit is necessary. Without profit a business cannot survive. It will not provide a return for the owners and investors who take risks to keep it going. Nor will it have resources to invest in further growth. Profit is not a dirty word!

But should profit be the primary goal of business? Saying profit is the goal of business is analogous to suggesting that the life goal of human beings is breathing, because without breathing we cannot survive. It also suggests that the ultimate purpose of business is survival; but sometimes actions need to be taken because they are right and not because they are profitable. Sometimes these costly choices can cause a business to die.

Christians have other difficulties with using profit and money as the ultimate goal for our own lives and as the primary goal of business. The Bible cautions against letting money making become a life purpose. The New Testament talks about the dangers of money more than any other subject except the Kingdom of God. Money can be used for good. But it also has the power to demand loyalty and allegiance. "What good will it be for a man if he gains the whole world, yet forfeits his soul? . . ." (Matthew 16:26). We must have a higher purpose than making money.

The ability of a business to make a profit does not determine if products are socially beneficial. Goods and services that are harmful, create envy, or result in poor stewardship can all be profitable. Pornography, manufacturing alcoholic beverages, and producing and distributing illegal drugs are very profitable. Yet none of us would want to make our living in those businesses. If profitability is the chief end of business, any item that can be marketed can be justified if it is profitable. The simple fact that someone will buy a product is not enough justification for Christians to produce it.

The level of short-term profit is also an incomplete indicator of the effectiveness, efficiency, or well-being of a business. A number of other important indicators are more important for the long term: employee satisfaction, relationships with dealers and suppliers, careful use of scarce resources, ethical relationships to competitors, and respect from customers are a few examples. A business can look good when measured by short-term profitability, yet be weak underneath.

Since profit making alone is a shallow and limited goal for Christians in business, what are some other goals worthy of committed Christians? Look at the Point for Discussion. You'll see at least four ways to extend God's shalom in business:

1. *To provide goods and services that enhance the lives of individuals and society.* Christians who truly believe they're making better vacuum cleaners or more reliable, fuel-efficient cars can be serving God's kingdom. Their primary purpose, however, is not profit, but service to individuals and society.

2. *To create and maintain jobs.* What better way to serve God than to create meaningful work for people? Work that supports families financially and psychologically and harnesses their creative energies is kingdom work.

3. *To provide a fair return for committed investors and owners.* Increasing the wealth of shareholders is not a company's only goal, but it is an appropriate goal because of the risks investors have taken. Returns to owners also provide family income or retirement security. It is a way of rewarding them for the venture of capitalizing the business.

4. *The allocation of business resources to community projects.* Businesses can use their talents to support worthy charities, improve the culture of their community, support higher education, or contribute to a host of other social needs.

For Christians the relevant question is how to best balance these multiple goals. Christians in business should work hard to develop very successful businesses because that gives them increased opportunities to serve. They might, for example, develop a great network of music stores or become the most efficient VCR producer. But they do it for a much larger range of reasons than to simply make the largest possible profit.

So, then, what about profits? Making a profit is not wrong. No business can survive very long without making a profit. But profit is a means to other goals rather than an end in itself. It allows the company to stay alive so that it can accomplish its kingdom service. Profits provide rewards to employees and investors. They are a source of finances for community projects. They allow for growth. Profits are one indicator for measuring efficiency and effectiveness. But for Christians, profits are means, not ends!

Many non-Christians share these objectives. Some of them also recognize profits as means to serve humanity. The mission statement of Johnson and Johnson, emphasizing services to customers, employees, communities, and stockholders, exemplifies values clearly compatible with those of Christians. But we must go further to link our goals with God's. For Christians growing profits expand our stewardship responsibility. They increase temptation for misuse, but they also open many opportunities to serve God by serving our neighbors.

Regulation of Business

There is always a tension between individual freedom, which is valued highly in our society, and the need to limit freedom for the common good. This tension expresses itself at the individual and institutional levels. We want to be free to do as we please, but sometimes exercising our freedom harms others. Similarly businesses do not like government control or laws that restrict their freedom. Yet sometimes those restrictions are necessary to protect society from harmful consequences.

Control is of two kinds, internal and external. Any reasonable driver tries to drive at a safe speed because of a desire to stay alive and out of concern for other drivers. This self-control regulates and restricts the driver's freedom. At the same time there are laws that set limits. These laws are society's way of enforcing limits on those who do not have adequate self-control. It is society's way of expressing a consensus on the maximum safe speed. Even those who have a lot of self-control sometimes need the threat of a flashing blue light as a reminder to do what is right!

Biblically self-control is a fruit of the Spirit (Galatians 5:23). This is very significant because, by reverse logic, those who do not live by the Spirit would not be expected to exercise as much self-control.

Without it businesspeople easily rationalize that if an action is not illegal, it is acceptable. Such an attitude invites government regulation, because it inherently depends on the law to establish moral boundaries. In our world we cannot depend on self-control alone to regulate business.

Therefore business needs regulation that is a combination of self-control and societal controls. Self-control begins with the moral commitments of business professionals. These values are reflected in their formal business policies. In recent years many businesses have adopted codes of ethics and statements of social responsibility. Many colleges teach business ethics courses, and ethics is also a hot topic on the consulting circuit. Business has recognized the problems caused when sound moral values are not promoted in their organizations.

Greater self-control creates less need for government regulation. Yet government is society's agent for imposing external controls and for enforcing the social contract. At its best government represents the interest of all people and is particularly concerned for those with special needs. But in the real world government is subject to manipulation by special interest groups and to power plays by individuals in the legislature and the current administration. It sometimes serves itself rather than the broad interests of the people.

Christians need to examine their views of government regulation of business. Many of us rather glibly suggest that the least government is the best government. That is far too simple an answer. Government is one way that people in a country do things together. It is also a way of taking care of things that no one person or group can take care of themselves. We need to recognize the positive roles government can play in partnership with business.

It is not possible to allow the same freedom of choice and experimentation in a high-tech, urban society that existed in a rural, agricultural society. Risks of harm are greater today in heavily populated urban areas than in sparsely populated rural areas. Nearly everything we do affects other people. Society should have a larger voice in matters that hold potential public risks even when these grow from the private sector. For example, the operation of the nuclear energy industry would be inconceivable without government regulation and inspection.

Although there are no easy answers to questions about the role of government, several principles are clear. First, God has instituted the function of government to regulate society and to see that broad interests are served. Therefore Christians are to respect the government and try to change it to better serve society as God intended. Second, government is a mechanism to do things as a group that cannot be done as well individually— building roads or water systems, or going to the moon. Third, within a free enterprise system, government has a particular responsibility to maintain fair competition and to protect the rights of people who cannot compete. Fourth, Christians are to live by higher principles than society's law. Simply doing the minimum the law requires is not enough.

We Christians in business would be wiser spending our time shaping government's partnership with us than resisting it. Regulations on safety, taxation, pricing, advertising, and a host of other activities are necessary for the common good. They can restrain evil and advise us of limits. However, the best regulations, those that really serve their purpose, are ones formulated with our help. We have the daily experience and are closest to many of those affected by them. As Christians we should serve their interests by helping to shape careful, efficient, and effective regulations.

Questions for Reflection

Our Mission in Business

1. How do you respond to the statement at the beginning of the chapter? Do you agree that business can be mission?
2. Dennis Bakke is the executive vice president of Alternative Energy Systems, Inc., a large company providing electricity to

a number of cities. He proposes that churches hold commissioning services for businesspeople just as they do for missionaries. Churches should also hold businesspeople accountable by periodically asking them to report how they are building the Kingdom of God in their business. What do you think of these ideas?

3. Can business be both part of God's mission to the world and be profitable?

Exploring the Bible

1. Read Genesis 1:1–31 and 2:15. Focus on verses 26 to 31 of Chapter 1. Build on this passage to develop a set of principles for business as a steward of God's creation.

Contemporary Comment

1. The chapter suggests that business operates with an implied "social contract" with society. Make two lists. On one, list those things that society expects from business. On the other, list the things that business can expect from society.

2. How can the opportunities for less powerful groups in society to enforce their rights in the social contract be increased?

3. Discuss the roles for government listed just before the summary of the chapter. Critique these. Suggest others. How can the government fill these functions?

NOTES

1. Wally Kroeker, "Business as Mission," *The Marketplace* (January/February 1988): 8. Reprinted with permission.

Chapter 17

SOCIAL RESPONSIBILITY AS STEWARDSHIP

NCR's Mission: To Create Value

At NCR we've found that in order to create value, we must first satisfy the legitimate expectations of every person with a stake in our company. We call these persons our stakeholders, and we attempt to satisfy their expectations by promoting partnerships in which everyone is a winner.

Stakeholders

We believe in building mutually beneficial and enduring relationships with all our stakeholders based on conducting business activities with integrity and respect.

Customers

We take customers' satisfaction personally: we are committed to providing superior value in our products and services on a continuing basis.

Employees

We respect the individuality of each employee and foster an environment in which employees' creativity and productivity are encouraged, recognized, valued, and rewarded.

Suppliers

We think of our suppliers as partners who share our goal of achieving the highest quality standards and the most consistent level of service.

Communities

We are committed to being caring and supportive corporate citizens within the worldwide communities in which we operate.

Shareholders

We are dedicated to creating value for our shareholders and financial communities by performing in a manner that will enhance returns on investments.[1]

Stakeholding and Stewardship

In the past a businessperson who made a profit, provided an acceptable place of work, paid a going wage, and obeyed the law was considered to have done a good job. No longer. Henry Ford II recognized this when he told students and faculty of the Harvard Business School in 1969, "The terms of the contract between industry and society are changing. . . . Now we are being asked to serve a wider range of human values and to accept an obligation to members of the public with whom we have no commercial transactions."[2]

Ford recognized that business is intricately interrelated with the rest of its community and world. No individual business can exist in a vacuum. It needs employees from its community. It needs police and fire protection and stable government. It uses water and air and natural resources that belong to everybody. Each business has a responsibility to its community to be a good steward of resources, to be a good neighbor, and to work in ways that contribute to the total welfare of the community. Business is a social institution. It joins with other social institutions such as the family in doing its part to enhance life and meet needs of people. This is often called social responsibility.

NCR takes very seriously its responsibility to its neighbors. In the Point for Discussion NCR calls all the people and groups affected by its actions "stakeholders." It recognizes that many diverse parties hold a stake in NCR because they are affected by the way NCR conducts its business. As Christians we can affirm that perspective. Recognizing that all of these diverse publics have a stake in a company really does make a difference in how NCR operates.

Christians add an additional dimension. God ultimately owns everything (Leviticus 25:23). God has given us the responsibility to manage the earth and all of its resources to provide every person a meaningful and productive life. God gives us freedom, within guidelines, to make decisions—even wrong ones—in administering God's property. With that freedom comes responsibility: as stewards we must account to God for the choices we make on God's behalf.

Christians are called to exercise their stewardship responsibility to God by managing their businesses in ways that serve the needs of their communities. Previous chapters have considered responsibilities to shareholders and employees. Let's now consider our stewardship responsibilities to customers, competitors, community, and the environment.

Responsibility Toward Customers

A key issue in our responsibility toward customers is the decision about what we make and sell. Most of us would not be involved in illegal or obviously immoral products and services. These do not benefit customers even though they might want to buy them. We would not want to be in the business of selling cocaine or publishing pornography. However, most issues are more subtle than those. Is it appropriate to create and sell nonessential goods and services that customers want but don't really need? Even asking the question that way assumes that we know which goods and services are needed and which ones are not. It is also very important to analyze which human needs and drives we appeal to in making a sale. Pricing is another issue. What are the relationships between the price of products, their quality, and "truth"?

First, let's look at the relationship between wants and needs. The eyes of humankind are never satisfied, says the wisdom writer (Proverbs 27:20). No matter how much we have, we want more. This continual desire is often exploited by advertisers. Christians need to raise serious questions about whether or not it is right to create products and stimulate new desires simply to make money.

Separating real needs from wants is not easy in our own lives nor in the broader society. Are things like perfumed soap, deodorant, computers, designer clothes, spiffy cars, and endless shelves of books needs or wants? How do we tell? Do we exercise good stewardship only when we produce and sell essentials?

One of the virtues of the market system is its freedom to support or discourage the creativity of producers. Many items are advertised today as "products for the person who has everything." In his book *The Affluent Society* John Kenneth Galbraith called this type of advertising "want creation" because it is a never-ending treadmill encouraging consumption to stimulate production. As a society we want a stable economy, thereby protecting jobs. So it is tempting to encourage business to make and sell anything and everything a consumer will buy.

God created us to enjoy life. God wants us to have more than the bare essentials. Not all wants are bad, just because they are non-essentials. A good piano, a piece of fine art, or a new suit are not absolutely essential, yet they do enhance life. As Christians we must make choices regarding the products and services we create and promote. Our emphasis should be on products that produce lasting benefit and that really enhance life rather than on those that simply respond to status wants and consumer orientation.

Some people are satisfied to let the market decide this issue. If a product sells they assume that the price reflects the product's value and that it meets some legitimate need. Many rationalize that government regulations protect consumers against really unsafe products. They answer the questions about what products should be made and sold by delegating responsibility to consumer choices with a dash of government intervention.

As Christians in business we should not let ourselves off the hook so easily. If we are producers and marketers, we make choices regarding which needs and wants to appeal to. We use resources under our stewardship to carry out those decisions. We must be as responsible for those choices as are individual consumers. We can choose to make and sell luxury cars or family sedans, educational toys, or pet rocks. How do we make such choices?

The answers to these questions related to a particular product are often not clear-cut, but there are some useful principles. First, the product should do something positive, such as enhancing the physical and psychological well-being of those who buy it. On such a basis we would rule out the creation and sale of toys that promote violence. We should consider whether or not a product has substantial potential for harm. Virtually all products have some potential for harm, of course, but those risks must be balanced against the potential for good. Cars are dangerous, for example, but the benefits outweigh that danger. Cigarettes might be judged differently.

We should also look at the primary purpose the product fills. A product's primary intention should not be the creation of status for the buyers and envy for those who cannot afford it. Items that encourage covetousness only because of their snob appeal should be evaluated carefully by Christian producers. Such concern should discourage us from entering industries heavily involved in goods and services that are used specifically to flaunt wealth. Marketing $20,000 fur coats, for example, might give us some second thoughts.

Finally, we must be concerned about products that use resources inefficiently or create problems because of difficulties in disposing of them. Our increased use of disposable products that are not biodegradable is creating massive problems because there are not enough landfills in which to dispose of them. The problems of finding suitable places to store nuclear wastes have increased dramatically in recent years.

Christians have a special responsibility to develop and produce products that serve real needs and do not create new problems.

It is important to avoid simplistic responses to these issues. It is not enough to suggest that we fill needs and reject wants. God's blessings go far beyond merely meeting our physical needs. The issue cannot be simplified to a concern with frivolous trinkets or amusements. Looked at in isolation these are harmless. However, we must ask, "Given the resources at my disposal, what are the most valuable goods and services I can produce and market as a steward and servant?"

It is particularly important to take a global view in thinking about these issues. In many areas in the world people do not have enough to eat. Many places lack the basic necessities of pure water, clean air, and clothes to wear. It does not seem right that efforts are diverted to developing, producing, and selling frivolous and luxury goods in some countries while such basic needs exist in others.

In addition to the product itself it is important to examine the appeal that is used to generate a market. We need only to look a short time at magazine racks or TV before we encounter appeals to sex, beauty, success, power, and personal indulgence. Advertising implies that purchasing the product will guarantee acceptance, success, personal pleasure, or other valued ends that accompany the purchase. The pressures to buy are subtle and pervasive. Following them is a bit like drinking saltwater to satisfy thirst. The more we drink, the thirstier we get.

There are many good desires to which we can appeal. We need not stimulate the egocentric, lustful, and perverted ones. Many companies do appeal to wholesome associations between products and people. Some automobile ads promote features that increase auto safety. An insurance company promotes the community service activities of its employees. Some advertisements for food products emphasize health considerations. These advertisements appeal to positive consumer interests. Advertisements that give facts which help the buyer determine product features and quality also appeal to more appropriate motives.

Businesses should approach customers as people of dignity whom they genuinely want to serve. From God's perspective the purpose of business transactions is to serve people. To do this requires that direct selling approaches, sales promotions, and mass ads should be honest and appeal openly to healthy desires.

In addition to the product itself and the way it is promoted, it is important to find pricing strategies that reflect integrity and honesty.

The Maytag Corporation built its fine reputation over the years by building quality products for which customers were willing to pay a premium price. They established a quality/price relationship that was understood and accepted in the marketplace. Their reputation remains high because they continue to honor the implicit contract they made with their customers. Companies like Maytag encourage other organizations to develop reasonable quality/price relationships for their products.

Because many companies face real pressures to keep prices as low as possible, they are tempted to cut quality in ways that cheat customers. In a prayer from *Bless This Desk: Prayers 9 to 5* Ken Thompson writes:

> SOMEBODY'S GOING TO GET STUCK
> They say, God, that our old standard Model 17HL
> isn't showing the profit it should.
> (Still, its popularity is holding well.)
> The fellows in the plant
> say they can reduce the special machining
> and use a lighter metal for the frame,
> adding thirty percent more profit for us!
> Now, that's well and good
> (Those guys are trained for such as this.)
> But, who should speak for the customers, Lord?
> They're going to get less and pay the same.

It doesn't seem right
but it does seem like good business!
Thirty percent
or thirty pieces of silver? Amen. [3]

The statement, "It doesn't seem right, but it does seem like good business!" expresses the tension many of us feel. We feel the pressures to maintain profitability by making short-run tradeoffs between price and quality.

These pressures are complicated even further by competitors' pricing strategies, which may bear little relationship to product costs. Prices may be set high to manipulate consumer perceptions that high prices indicate premium products. Conversely prices may be set low to function as loss leaders, to drive others out of business, or to prevent other businesses from entering the market.

In setting prices we must consider variable and fixed costs, the need for research and development, and a reasonable profit margin. These factors have to be taken into account. They do not contradict biblical principles governing such situations which forbid intentional quality price deception. Reputations become implied contracts to which customer expectations are tied. We must be honest in price setting, reflecting product values in the prices we set. Such policies show love for our customer neighbors; deceiving and taking advantage of them does not.

Responsibility Toward Competitors

Both the buyer and the seller should benefit from any sale. According to this principle of mutual benefit there are no winners and losers. When sellers compete with each other, however, it's a different story. Both sellers cannot get the sale. One wins; the other loses. Therefore getting the sale probably raises more ethical issues than any other single activity in business.

Competition is what runs the marketplace. In Michael Porter's *Competitive Strategy*, one of the premier academic studies on competition in business, the author develops a model that describes the interplay between insecurity and power. Within this framework all businesses are both sellers and buyers. Business sellers constantly strive to stave off the insecurity of new competitors trying to enter the market and provide substitute products. Buyers in business have a countervailing set of power strategies to protect themselves from the influence of sellers. On the one hand they seek strategies to dominate and control. On the other hand they perfect defenses to prevent being dominated and controlled by rivals. Porter's theory shows the various strategies available to businesses for managing competition.

Competition in business is keen. The pressures to win are enormous. The individual whose identity depends on sales success has a lot at stake. The accompanying tension can even prompt irresponsible and dishonest behavior. Several years ago a major aircraft manufacturer bribed high level foreign government officials to secure an order. Another company executive planted public seeds of doubt about a competitor's product safety.

Financially strong companies have been known to price products below cost and absorb losses in order to destroy weaker companies that could not sustain losses. Some companies engage in illegal espionage to steal secrets from other companies. Some companies attempt to hire highly skilled employees or employees with special knowledge from other companies. Negative advertising designed to destroy the reputations of opponents has become commonplace in business campaigns.

Christians in business do have responsibilities to their competitors. These can take many forms. Recently a poultry processing plant in central Virginia experienced a fire. It was forced to suspend production for some time. This could have caused major problems. The company's growers had large numbers of turkeys ready for processing; its markets were expecting the delivery of products. Employees needed work. For some competitors that misfortune could have provided a great opportunity. They might have moved aggressively into the markets left undersupplied, or tried to buy birds from the growers at low prices.

The firm's largest competitor across town did neither of these things. Since it was not using its processing line second and third shifts, it offered to allow the firm that had the fire to bring in its employees during these shifts and continue processing turkeys. That kind of help to a competitor is to be affirmed and admired.

Most of the principles that should guide the relationships of Christian businesspersons to their competitors grow from commitments to integrity and honesty. It is clear that we should never undermine a competitor by using derogatory hearsay to cast suspicion on their operations. Unfounded insinuations, such as, "I understand that Product Z is not holding up well and that maintenance costs are way out of hand after eighteen months," are not ethical. God does not like gossip, rumor spreading, or false innuendo. All forms of deception to gain unfair advantage are wrong. Even if such an assertion is documented by independent and unbiased sources, it is not morally defensible to intentionally hurt a competitor.

One of the great deficiencies of competition is the waste of energy spent devising strategies to respond to competitors rather than to work with our own strengths. Often spending energy attending to our customers' needs would prove far more productive than attempting to counter every move by a competitor.

We cannot ignore competitors and relevant information about their products. But we use such data to improve our own service to customers, not to intentionally hurt our rivals. We owe our competitors respect and kindness: they too are created in the image of God. Positive effort toward improving our own service or product is more appropriate than criticizing and downgrading our competitors.

Responsibility Toward Community

As Christians in business we need to be involved in our communities, not merely to keep up good appearances but to represent Christ's concerns for justice and kindness. Hershey Corporation in

Hershey, Pennsylvania, includes in their statement of values a desire to be a good neighbor. This means contributing to community projects, encouraging Hershey executives to volunteer for community projects and boards, and trying to monitor the impact of the company on the community. Hershey is very much concerned about its impact on the environment.

This recognition of a company's responsibility to be a good neighbor encourages a company to be concerned for the welfare of the entire community, and not only things that affect the company directly. Companies have power. They should use it in appropriate ways to work for good schools, good housing, good zoning, and other programs that will enhance the community. Unfortunately some companies use their power only to protect themselves and keep their taxes low. This is shortsighted.

Christians in business should balance power with responsibility. It is reasonable to monitor whether tax dollars are used to benefit the general citizenry effectively. The company has a responsibility to pay the property, sales, and income taxes regularly and without complaint.

Businesses should seek what is fair and just for all segments of the community. They should not seek benefits for business that work to the detriment of other community interests. Suppose a business wants a railroad spur funded in large measure by local public funds extended to its back door. The business should be sure that it can document real benefits in economic growth for the whole community, not just added dividends for out-of-town shareholders. In the public forum, business must learn to balance its own interests with those of other parties.

Business must realize that it does often have a disproportionate level of power to influence decisions. Private conversations with public officials about community issues are often preferable to public pronouncements. A private setting provides room for the public officials to listen, discuss, and explore realities "off the record." Those who govern should be encouraged to do what is just and to listen to all community segments. Although as business leaders we should support healthy community programs and standards, doing so as quiet partners may be the best approach.

Communities may need more than quiet support. They often need money and employees' time for special community projects. Community schools, parks, recreation programs, health services for the disadvantaged, and a host of other projects need help from business. Company foundations that provide money and employee time back up concern with hands-on effort.

We should remember that we serve not only local, but state, national, and global communities. Although we cannot be all things to all communities, we should remember that our obligations for justice do not stop at the city limits signs but extend to taking leadership in finding peaceful and just solutions to global issues.

Responsibility for the Environment

In the 1960s interest in environmental and ecological issues exploded. We began to hear about "Spaceship Earth." Business-people contemplated the limited supply of resources. We began to worry about the greenhouse effect of atmospheric ozone changes, which could warm the earth, melt the polar ice caps, raise the sea levels, and alter weather patterns. We also began to express concern over the possible extinction of various plants and animals. We began to worry about scarring the earth with pit mining, defoliation, acid rain, and groundwater pollution.

Numerous concerns stem from the interaction of business technologies with the environment. We must find places to store nuclear waste created by the energy industry. We must reduce the amount of acid rain resulting from manufacturing processes. Chemical wastes that result from industrial production must be safely processed.

Unfortunately some Christians in business, when criticized for their environmental abuse, have responded that they are free to do what they want because God has given them dominion over the earth (Genesis 1:28–30). Their lack of concern is tragic; but it is even more tragic that they invoke the name of God to justify irresponsible stewardship. Genesis speaks of dominion not for exploitation, but for cultivation and caring for God's world (Genesis 2:15).

Other biblical statements about the created world are also applicable to our high-tech society. We can say with certainty that God is interested in how we manage depletable resources. When the people of God were in an agrarian culture, God explained in considerable detail how they should let the land lie fallow and rest. It was only three thousand years later that we discovered how wise and scientifically correct these commands were (Exodus 23:10–11; Leviticus 25:1–7).

God is also concerned with our respect for animal life. Proverbs informs us that "a righteous man cares for the needs of his animal . . ." (12:10). Everything God created has a purpose. Every bird, every fish, and every mammal should be treated with awe. When we destroy animal habitats and provide no other alternatives, we have not respected God's creation.

Contamination that threatens human health is a concern of God as well. The Old Testament concept of shalom—living in harmony with God, our neighbors, and the created order—is deeply violated by pollutants that affect humans. When we are concerned for human health and safety we are showing respect for the sanctity of human life. Even the home builder in Israel was told, "When you build a new house, you shall make a parapet for your roof, that you may not bring bloodguilt on your house if anyone fall from it" (Deuteronomy 22:8 NASB). It seems inconceivable that someone would overlook the importance of safe and healthy human environments, yet many people do.

The biggest hindrances to proper stewardship of the environment are ignorance, impatience, and greed. The technological explosion has outrun our understanding of its consequences and side effects. Many harmful consequences occurred before we were aware that the products were dangerous to land, animal, and human environments. We are now learning that every new technology has the potential for vast areas of dangerous ignorance.

In the competitive market time has a dollar value. We are under great pressure to move quickly before a competitor does. This creates impatience, which in turn may lead to environmental dangers. Food and drug regulations, for example, were initially passed in 1906 to require the labeling of additives in processed food; but it was not until 1958 that the law was amended to require pre-market testing of additives to see if they were safe for humans. Our technical ability to produce new products, coupled with competitive pressures to get to the market first, provides the urge to act on untested presumptions.

In the recent past, as managers sought greater market share and higher profit levels, greed often outweighed care for the environment. It is now heartening to see many companies taking evimental issues seriously. Christians should be concerned for the environment as a matter of good stewardship. Applied Energy Services in Washington, DC, is an example of a firm that tries to take this concern seriously. It builds and operates efficient and relatively clean coal-burning plants to produce electricity. High-tech scrubbers and many other technological devices make sure the burning process is as clean as possible. Even so, the plants cannot expel totally clean air. Since trees restore oxygen to the air, each year Applied Energy Systems plants enough trees to purify a volume of air equal to the volume of air their high-tech scrubbers fail to clean up. This is one creative approach to environmental responsibility.

QUESTIONS FOR REFLECTION

NCR's Mission: To Create Value

1. Is it possible to create value for all of the stakeholders as NCR suggests, or must there be trade-offs?
2. Many Christian businesspeople include in their mission statements a goal "to honor God." In what ways is that statement similar and in what ways different from the NCR statement?

3. Can a perspective such as NCR's be promoted as "good business," or will it be too costly if followed seriously?

Exploring the Bible

1. One of the motives that drives people to selfishness rather than stewardship is insatiable wants. What do the following Scriptures have to say about simple lifestyle? Luke 1:46–53; Luke 12:22–31; 2 Corinthians 9:8–11; Luke 12:33–34; 1 Timothy 6:9–10; Luke 12:16–21.

Contemporary Comment

1. Discuss business activities such as leveraged buy-outs, stock trading, and other financial transactions that do not directly produce a product or service. Do these activities fit "stewardship" criteria? Why or why not?
2. Discuss some ways that business in America might exercise stewardship for generations not born and for people in other parts of the world.
3. One aspect of stewardship is giving to those with need and to the church. Several people have suggested a graduated tithe. One model would suggest 10 percent on the first $10,000 of income, 20 percent on the next $5,000, 30 percent on the next $5,000, and so on. What level of giving do you suggest?
4. In marketing products is it appropriate to foster "prestige" images? Is it right to build on perceived product differences when in fact there are none?

NOTES

1. This is a statement of NCR's mission to create value for all of its stockholders. First published in 1987. Used with permission of NCR Corp., 1700 South Patterson Blvd., Dayton, OH 45479.
2. Thomas Donaldson and Patricia Werhane, *Ethical Issues in Business* (Englewood Cliffs, NJ: Prentice Hall, 1983), 153.
3. Ken Thompson, *Bless This Desk: Prayers 9 to 5* (Nashville, TN: Abingdon Press, 1976), 59.

Chapter 18

JUSTICE AND THE WORLD'S WEALTH

Playing Monopoly ®: A Modern Parable

Playing Monopoly ®, the Parker Brothers kind, is fun. Besides throwing the dice, collecting the rent, and building hotels on Boardwalk, we get to decide which risks to take and which to avoid. On the one hand there is suspense and intrigue, and on the other there is safe predictability. All we need is a combination of luck and skill. But every Monopoly ® game turns out the same because one player gets rich and the others go broke.

As a game Monopoly ® is not to be taken seriously. It is a gross simplification of reality. Because of that simplification playing Monopoly ® can be used as a modern parable, a simple story with a deep meaning. Have you ever thought how you would play Monopoly ® with justice as your primary goal?

One approach is to focus on issues of personal morality. Don't smoke or drink. Be honest. Don't weight the dice. Count the money correctly. Don't gloat as you collect rent or buy hotels. Try hard, but don't be greedy. Invest your assets well. Pray as you pass "Go." Work hard even if you are losing. Share a bit now and then with players in need.

All of these things are very important, but practicing them does not change the outcome of the game. Someone gets rich and the others go broke. Many of these values are essential if the game is to work. After all, it is no fun if the people going broke quit.

Playing Monopoly ® justly must go beyond personal morality. It should have something to do with the way money is distributed. What choices really affect the distribution of money and power?

To act justly in Monopoly ® requires more than just personal morality; it requires playing by different rules. For example, what would happen if the rent for Boardwalk were cut in half? Or if the players could own only two houses? Or if everybody got $1,000 for passing "Go"? What would happen if each player were required to sell property at cost and start over every twenty turns? What other rules could be changed to alter the outcome? Is there a way to play so that everyone wins?

Every parable must be interpreted. In the game of economic life we are the players. The rules are the social and economic structures. God calls us to live justly and righteously. To do so requires more than personal morality. It requires living by different rules and changing those which do not promote justice. In life God calls us to find a way for everyone to win.

Sharing Wealth

Every Christian supports personal morality. Have you ever heard a Christian advocate dishonesty? Or seriously propose treating an employee in a nasty way? Probably not. The Point for Discussion makes the point that personal morality is important, but that we must go further. If we want to act justly we need to be concerned about structure and about the rules that govern such things as the way money and power are distributed. That is what this chapter is about.

Differences in wealth and resources between individuals and between nations disconcert us. It does not seem right that one family should have an income of several million dollars while another makes less than $10,000. Nor does it seem right that one country has a per capita income of $16,000 and another $500. Those disparities have many causes, but the structures that govern distribution of money and power are certainly at the core.

These differences have effects far beyond the maldistribution of money. Community members may psychologically withdraw from a family that amasses a great deal of wealth; or they may be constantly on that family's doorstep for charitable donations. Children in school sometimes make fun of children from poor families who cannot afford trendy clothes. Employees may feel frustrated when the CEO walks away with an annual salary and bonuses over a million dollars while they receive a five percent raise. The leaders of some less-developed nations suggest that rich nations have become rich because they extricated minerals and other wealth from poor nations without fair payment. Income and wealth differences at both the individual and national levels force us to consider our obligations to our neighbors in the distribution of wealth.

We must be careful in thinking about this issue because economic transactions don't necessarily result in a winner and a loser. Sometimes both parties benefit. We must also recognize that one person's unproductive rock field is another person's productive rock quarry. Differences in human talent and persistence contribute logically to different economic outcomes.

Most people don't think much about the economic system as long as they are doing well. They believe in systems that provide for them personally. Generally they evaluate economic policy in terms of its impact on themselves, and don't put the needs of others foremost in their thoughts. Rich and poor alike generally look out for their own interests, though the rich are usually more successful.

Working for narrow self-interest is not a peculiar affliction of those in business. It is found among people everywhere. The Apostle Paul understood this well when he sent Timothy to the Philippians and said, "I have no one else like him [to send] who takes a genuine interest in your welfare. For everyone looks out for his own interests, not those of Jesus Christ" (Philippians 2:19–21).

Greed also makes people forget the needs of others. In a selfish search for status and security, many people greedily go after wealth. Wealth appears to buy comfort, security, power, and reputation. These give feelings of self-fulfillment. Paul and Peter both recognized that greed could even permeate the work of those who labored in the name of Christ (1 Thessalonians 2:5; 2 Peter 2:2–3, 14).

Christ warns his followers, "Watch out! Be on your guard against all kinds of greed; a man's life does not consist in the abundance of his possessions" (Luke 12:15). When tempted by greed we should remember that God has given us all that we have in order to enhance life for everybody.

Out of gratitude for God's gifts we should be stewards of wealth for the benefit of others. Paul encouraged the believers in Corinth to give so that there would be equity. He encouraged those with plenty to supply the needy so that ". . . He that gathered much did not have too much, and he that gathered little did not have too little" (2 Corinthians 8:15). Sharing wealth, whether it be between family members, within a business entity, with future generations, within a nation, or between nations, is at the core of God's definition of justice.

In a world dominated by sin, where love for God and neighbors means little to so many people, it is important for Christians to work to create economic and political structures that share the wealth God has made available.

Individual Wealth

How much is enough? What level of differences in individual wealth should be allowed to exist? Under historic capitalism the accumulation of individual wealth acquired legally in a free market was allowed without community interference. Because individuals were allowed to possess whatever they could legally acquire, private property and inheritance were limited only by opportunity and personal effort.

Other countries limit the accumulation of personal wealth. A Communist system does this by abolishing private property. Many Socialist countries have a heavily graduated income tax and regulate rights of inheritance. Such structures stress income equality and discourage family accumulation of wealth. Wage structures are also different in different countries. In Japan, for example, high-level executives make far less than their counterparts in the United States.

Christians need to think very carefully about the issues of personal wealth. It is clear from the Bible that God is the title-holder of all creation (Leviticus 25:23; Psalms 50:10; 104:24). In this sense we know that nothing we own is really our own. All we possess is held in trust from God to be used to improve the quality of life for all people. We will need to account to God for our stewardship.

Paul writes to Timothy,

For we have brought nothing into the world, and we can take nothing out of it. But if we have food and clothing, we will be content with that. People who want to get rich fall into temptation and a trap and into many foolish and harmful desires that plunge men into ruin and destruction. For the love of money is the root of all kinds of evil. Some people, eager for money, have wandered from the faith and pierced themselves with many griefs. (1 Timothy 6:7–10)

Yet in prosperous times, with hard work, we may accumulate wealth as a by-product of our efforts. This brings many obligations. We are required to give generously to the needy in our own backyards and around the globe.

How much should we give? Paul, in writing to the Corinthians, suggests three guidelines for giving. First, our level of giving should reflect the sincerity of our love for Christ. Second, we should recognize our own legitimate needs, not giving beyond the point where we too would be hard-pressed. Third, the amount of the gift, even if small, should be acceptable. Paul writes, "Now finish the work, so that your eager willingness to do it may be matched by your completion of it, according to your means. For if the willingness is there, the gift is acceptable according to what one has, not according to what he does not have" (2 Corinthians 8:11–12).

We have so many opportunities for contributing to exciting causes when God has given us financial wealth. Giving to missions allows us to be part of sharing the gospel around the world. We can help train and equip Christians to serve by contributing to Christian colleges. In our own communities we have opportunities to help disabled children and adults and other needy people through organizations like the United Way. Wealth brings dangers and temptations, to be sure. It also brings opportunities to be a partner with God in extending God's kingdom and meeting the needs of less fortunate people. That is a great thrill.

Possessing wealth also opens many opportunities for service by investing that wealth in businesses that create products or provide needed services. For example, disposing of so-called "disposable" diapers is a serious problem because they do not decompose. One entrepreneur who has done well in other businesses has recently used skill to research and develop a way to recycle diapers into fence posts. In that application the diapers' indestructability becomes an asset. He already has a long list of other products he thinks can be created from garbage and throw-away plastics. The money he makes from manufacturing fence posts will be reinvested in further research and development. He has a contract to work at constructive uses of used styrofoam products.

Gaining personal wealth is not an adequate goal for Christians. But when God does give us wealth we are to use it as good stewards to increase the quality of life for others both by generous giving and thoughtful investment.

Democratization of Corporate Ownership

In most capitalistic countries wealth is not only accumulated by families, but also by corporations. Who should own and control corporate wealth?

In corporate America the historic answer is that stockholders own that wealth and govern corporate decisions. Yet that is not the whole story in practice. Many corporations put other interested parties on their boards, such as investment bankers, partners in large law firms representing the company, and major customers.

Unfortunately employees are rarely represented in corporate ownership and governance structures. This means that they do not have the opportunity to gain equity wealth, nor to influence company policies at the highest levels. Stockholders do have a right to influence company policies because their capital allows the company to exist. Employees also have a major stake. Their jobs are linked to the company's stability and profitability.

Many mergers and takeovers are done because of short-term financial benefits for stockholders. Often the impacts of such actions on the employees or the community in which the business is located are ignored. A number of people think that employees have a right to equity ownership and to the control it implies.

Within recent years there has been a fast-growing movement to develop Employee Stock Ownership Plans (ESOPS). There are well-defined federal regulations for ESOPS and a national association that advises employee-owned companies. Many companies include stock options in profit-sharing plans. Companies that encourage employee ownership do so both because they think it is a right for employees to share equity ownership and for more practical reasons.

Employee ownership tends to reduce the adversarial relationships that often exist between management and labor. Because ownership gives employees direct stake in the profitability of the company they tend to work harder and with more creativity. They tend to more freely share their ideas for increasing production or for new products. They also see the benefit of working in ways that benefit the entire company rather than just in ways that serve their own self-interest. In difficult times employee owners are more willing to make sacrifices for the welfare of the company than other employees.

As Christian business professionals we should welcome and advocate manager and worker ownership. Allowing workers and owners to share in the risks and fruits of their work promotes responsibility and accountability. Because every employee would have both a job and a portion of their savings at stake in the business, real interdependencies can be highlighted and servant leadership promoted.

Both for justice reasons and for practical reasons it seems appropriate to encourage employee equity ownership.

Resources for Future Generations

Preserving the potential of future generations to create wealth is also part of our understanding of justice. A great amount of wealth creation depends on the availability of natural resources. When we use these resources now we must carefully consider our responsibility to future generations.

When God gave us dominion over creation God also gave us freedom to consume and employ the resources provided, but within clear guidelines for careful stewardship. Waste, destruction, and harmful exploitation are not justified. We should not abuse God's trust.

Part of not abusing God's trust is being aware of our responsibility toward future generations to preserve natural resources. God demonstrated that land conservation is important by prescribing that the land was to lie fallow every seventh year, allowing it to rejuvenate (Exodus 23:10, 11; Leviticus 25:1–7).

God also made his interest in animals clear by very carefully instructing Noah to preserve two of every animal and seven of some (Genesis 6:19–7:4). God wanted to preserve not only the created human race, but the animal kingdom as well.

Many plant and animal resources replenish themselves if we provide healthy nurturing environments. Other natural resources, such as water, air, or aluminum, can be recycled. We can make synthetic fibers, rubber, or leather and substitutes for building materials, sources of energy, or ethical drugs. The resources at our disposal are abundant if we are careful and creative.

Unfortunately we do not know the limits of all the resources God has created. Technologies in hundreds of fields have not yet yielded all that they can. Yet we do know it is our duty to act for the provision of future generations. To do otherwise would impoverish and deny them their portion of God's blessings in creation.

Part of the responsibility to create justice includes a responsibility to use resources carefully.

The Gross National Product and a Just Economic System

In our country we always want more. In national policy this is expressed as a constant drive to increase the Gross National Product. On the personal level it is expressed by a constant drive to have more money in order to be able to buy more and to live better. Many people have falsely assumed that a larger personal income means a higher quality of life for themselves and that a higher GNP guarantees a higher quality of life for the country. Neither assumption is correct. Our high standard of living can and often does come at the expense of personal contentment, strong family life, and stable communities.

In national policy, if the drive to raise GNP is realized apart from genuine concerns for equity, it is an inappropriate goal. Just wages and an equitable distribution of wealth must accompany any rise in the GNP if it is to be considered worthwhile. It is immoral to justify any system that fosters a widening spread in the per capita wealth between those at the top and the bottom of the economic ladder, while ignoring the needs of those at the bottom (Isaiah 5:8–10). This has in fact happened in our country during the 1980s. Homelessness has increased. The percentage of children in poverty has increased. At the same time the number of very rich people has also increased. Throughout Scripture repeated concern is expressed for those who are disadvantaged through no fault of their own—the orphans, widows, poor, or sick. For this reason a just economic system should not create barriers that hinder some citizens' access to work, natural resources, and capital.

Christians must decide what economic policies best manage wealth to provide for the needs of all people. The system should first of all encourage responsible personal care for self and family (1 Thessalonians 4:11, 12; 1 Timothy 5:4, 8). The system should encourage personal and business beneficence toward those who suffer from natural disadvantages. Finally, if the private sector fails to provide for the disadvantaged, the system should encourage public responsibility for helping people to help themselves.

Increases in GNP need to be understood in light of the fact that God is the ultimate provider and should reflect good resource stewardship, while creating new products that add to genuine well-being. A rising GNP should be backed by a system that fosters substantial opportunities for work and creativity. But, beyond these considerations, economic systems that increase GNP should encourage sharing the society's accumulated wealth.

Responsibilities Toward Our Global Neighbors

Is it fair that a small percentage of the population in the United States consumes a large percentage of the world's wealth? What economic responsibilities do developed nations have for less-developed nations? There are differences between nations because of differences in cultural, worldview, geography, language, and political customs.

Suppose you were trying to work at economic development among the Bushmen in the desert of Botswana. In order to survive the harsh environment of the desert, they place high value on maintaining equality and on sharing everything they have. There are highly developed mechanisms to punish a member of the group who rises above the others economically. As a person from North

America, you assume that to develop economically individual entrepreneurs need to develop businesses. However, you soon discover that the Bushmen refuse to own goods or buildings or keep money in the bank unless everyone else has the same amount. As soon as an individual takes initiative and builds a bit of capital he gives it away. If he does not, he will become the butt of cruel jokes and will be shamed by laughter. You soon learn that your advice to build capital for reinvestment is rejected. What is taken for granted in North America is rejected by the Bushmen.

Despite such differences, when people in other nations desire help and we have the capacity to provide it, we should share. Our basic responsibility is twofold. First, we should assist in meeting immediate physical needs for food, clothing, and shelter. Second, we should help them become economically self-sufficient. The wide gulf between the have and have-not nations would be reduced considerably if structural and artificial barriers to self-sufficiency that block development opportunities were knocked down.

Wealthy corporations in industrial nations with high standards of living often acquire cheap natural resources from poor, less-developed nations with low standards of living. They depend on the fact that they can pay low wages to reduce the costs of raw materials.

It is important to recognize the factors that determine differences in national wealth. Countries with high per capita incomes and standards of living have several common denominators. First, those people who are capable and willing to work have realistic opportunities to share in the nation's wealth. In the United States, for example, there is a large middle class. Second, there is a worldview that values and rewards personal initiative. Third, the legal system protects the rewards of personal accomplishments. Fourth, there is an infrastructure of utilities, transportation, and communication. Fifth, efforts must be undergirded by some awareness of the large-scale economic and political forces at work in the marketplace. Sixth, there is political stability. Finally, land and related natural resources are available to a wide segment of the population.

In biblical times the division of the Promised Land and the Jubilee principle were both means to accomplish this. Yet today the absence of broadly distributed land ownership is one of the major deterrents to the development of higher standards of living in less-developed nations. Much of the untapped wealth in this world is controlled by a few large landowners. Ignoring redistribution of concentrated wealth is a major barrier to economic growth. It prevents improvements in the standard of material well-being for masses of people.

Proponents of extensive socialism and communism promise redistribution of wealth by state action; but typically the state ends up owning and controlling the wealth. A wealthy class of bureaucrats often emerges. These systems have often not been creative or productive in underdeveloped nations because they lack the capacity to prepare broad groups within the cultures for meaningful economic responsibility. Communism has not produced the panacea it promised.

Justice requires that we genuinely try to encourage those with economic power to develop the skill and resource base of the working populace. Such development may create opportunities for them to raise their quality of life. In addition, a company that extracts natural resources should, as much as possible, encourage the reinvestment of their payments in capital good and capital-creating assets. Natural resources should be treated as capital, not as consumable income. Encouraging the exchange of capital for capital preserves the value of the exchange for future generations. Without such an exchange we exploit an advantage for one generation at the expense of another.

Governments, individual wealth-holders, and multinational corporations in underdeveloped nations should be encouraged to share. Exploitation of people or their natural resources should not continue. Christians in multinational corporations should seek to foster equity in less-developed nations and positively assist them in reaching their business potential. Economic activity is to be mutually beneficial. God's stewards should not exploit one country to benefit another.

QUESTIONS FOR REFLECTION

Playing Monopoly ®: A Modern Parable

1. What are some of the changes in the rules that would make the game more just?
2. Would the game be fun and would people play if wealth were distributed equally? Why or why not?
3. Why do those who are winning play with more enthusiasm than those who are losing?
4. Make applications to the real world. What can be learned?

Exploring the Bible

1. Read Leviticus 25 as if it were an economic policy proposed by the president to reorganize the economy. It suggests that every fifty years:

   • the soil is to lie fallow
   • debts are to be forgiven
   • slaves are to be freed
   • capital is to be redistributed by returning land to the families that originally owned it

   What would be some of the results of this policy? Would you support it? Why or why not? Could it be implemented?

Contemporary Comment

1. How do you respond to the following statement by Warren Braun, a pioneer in the development of stock ownership plans and president of Comsonics, a manufacturer of equipment used for installing and testing cable TV systems: "I sincerely believe that part of what people earn by doing their jobs is the right to participate in the ownership of the company."[1]
2. Donald Trump, the New York City real estate developer, writes in *Trump: The Art of the Deal*:

   A decision has been made to go into production on two Cadillac-body limousines using my name. The Trump Golden Series will be the most opulent stretch limousine made. The Trump Executive Series will be a slightly less lavish version of the same car. Neither one has yet come off the line, but the folks at Cadillac Motors Division recently sent over a beautiful gold Cadillac Allante as a gift. Perhaps they felt I needed more toys to keep me busy.[2]

When is enough enough? How do North American Christians determine an appropriate lifestyle when most of the world is poor?

3. The chapter suggests that one of the reasons North Americans have relatively inexpensive goods is that they get cheap natural resources and cheap labor from poor nations. Do you agree? Can or should this be changed?

NOTES

1. Warren Braun, Washington Business, *The Washington Post* (August 22, 1983).
2. Donald Trump, *Trump: The Art of the Deal* (New York: Random House, 1987), 239.

Chapter 19

BIBLICAL ABSOLUTES IN A WORLD OF CHANGE

Business Bluffing

In 1968 Albert Carr wrote a fascinating article in *Harvard Business Review*. The article, quite rightly, generated a storm of protest from businesspeople.

Carr argued that, while businesspeople are not indifferent to ethics in their private lives, in their office lives they cease to be private citizens. They become game players who must be guided by somewhat different ethical standards. He claimed that a lot can be learned about business by comparing it to a game of poker.

No one expects poker to be played on the ethical principles preached in churches. In poker it is right and proper to bluff a friend out of the rewards of being dealt a good hand . . . It is up to the other fellow to protect himself.

Poker has its special ethics, and here I am not referring to the rules against cheating. The man who keeps an ace up his sleeve, or who marks the cards is more than unethical; he is a crook, and can be punished as such—kicked out of the game, or in the old West, shot. . . .

Poker's own brand of ethics is different from the ethical ideals of civilized human relationships. The game calls for distrust of the other fellow. It ignores the claim of friendship. Cunning deception and concealment of one's strength and intentions, not kindness and openheartedness, are vital in poker.

No one thinks any the worse of poker on that account. And no one should think any worse of the game of business because its standards of right and wrong differ from the prevailing traditions of morality in our society.

To be a winner, a man must play to win. This does not mean that he must be ruthless, harsh, or treacherous. On the contrary, the better his reputation for integrity, honesty, and decency, the better his chances of victory in the long run. But from time to time every businessman, like every poker player, is offered the choice between certain loss or bluffing within the rules of the game. If he is not resigned to losing, if he wants to rise in his company and industry, then in such a crisis he will bluff—and bluff hard.[1]

Forces Undermining Absolutes

Concepts of right and wrong no longer seem to be operative in our society. Greed is justified because it helps the economy. Cheating on income tax is justified because everybody does it. Lying in political campaigns is accepted because it gets votes. Sins are not sins but shortcomings. One wag commented that if the Ten Commandments were written today they would be called the Ten Suggestions.

Is Albert Carr right? Does business have its own way of defining truth?

Modern secular philosophies such as materialism, relativism, skepticism, and pragmatism put human knowledge and experience at the center of reality. Materialism denies any reality beyond the physical dimensions of matter and life. Relativism says truth depends only on the situation and on your point of view. Skepticism denies that truth in moral matters can be known. Pragmatism proclaims that whatever works is acceptable. These philosophies suggest that there is no absolute truth about moral matters.

These philosophies and the realization that situations continually change give rise to the belief that there are no unchanging moral standards. Some people think that those who believe in absolutes are narrow, naive, closed-minded, and insecure anti-intellectuals. According to the Bible this perception is nothing new. At the time of Jesus' trial Pilate asked sarcastically, "What is truth?" (John 18:38).

Moral absolutes are also undermined because of the constant changes in science. As new information becomes available, theories change. Old theories are abandoned, new ones emerge. God wants us to continually learn more about the natural world. Our understanding is always incomplete, so we construct models to help us understand how science operates. Some people transfer this way of thinking to moral matters. They find it impossible to believe in absolute spiritual truths because scientific truth continues to change (1 Corinthians 2:14–16).

Christians who believe in the authority of Scripture are sometimes criticized by secular intellectuals as simple, unrealistic people who need not be taken too seriously. On the other hand, some Christians avoid testing their faith and belief in the authority of Scripture with rational thought or intellectual argument because they fear that it won't stand the test.

Believing in the authority of Scripture and following its commands do not require Christians to be intellectually naive or irrational. God has given us our intellects to use. We learn a great deal about the Bible and about God by using the tools of analysis and philosophy. We must remember, however, that our faith is in God and not in our own intellectual constructions or rational arguments. Those can become false gods and prevent us from hearing the Holy Spirit teach us of God.

Jesus tells us to love God with all our mind (Matthew 22:37). Using the rational faculties God has given us to defend our beliefs does not reduce faith to doubt; it enhances faith. To be rational merely means we can order thoughts so our interpretation of the world and events in it conforms to God's perspective on reality.

Every Christian must continually work to maintain the link between faith and reason. We should be ". . . destroying speculations and every lofty thing raised up against the knowledge of God, and [be] taking every thought captive to the obedience of Christ" (2 Corinthians 10:5 NASB). We are to "see to it that no one takes [us] captive through philosophy and empty deception, according to the tradition of men, according to the elementary principles of the world, rather than according to Christ" (Corinthians 2:8 NASB).

If Albert Carr is right about business bluffing, then business ethics is simply a matter of playing by the established rules of the game rather than following absolute moral rules. He doesn't ask about the structure of the game, the justice of the rules, or who invented them. As Christians we should not simply accept the rules of business as we find them. We look beyond them to the moral principles that God has established. These apply to business and to all areas of life.

Absolute Truth and Morality

Even though we are created in the image of God we are not the source of absolute truths about character, morality, or standards of conduct. God did not say to Adam and Eve, "Go forth and discover by experimentation what is right and wrong concerning human relationships in the various social, economic, political, and religious arrangements you may establish. Let trial and error become your moral teachers. You must discover the moral principles in the same way you are to discover the physical laws governing the material realm. Good luck; I will see you on the day of judgment."

No! Our first parents were asked to obey God's commands perfectly. When they did not obey God punished them. God called the patriarchs to obedience and gave Israel the Ten Commandments and emphasized moral justice through the prophets. Finally, and most important, God sent Jesus to model moral perfection.

When we assert that there are moral absolutes, we are not making claims about ourselves or our moral infallibility. Rather we are acknowledging that God is eternal and that morality emerges from

God's nature. The Bible teaches us about God and about the moral standards God has established.

Many people fear that this understanding of moral absolutes leads to the promulgation of cold, rigid, unyielding, lifeless laws. They think absolute moral standards cannot be changed to meet the unique situations of contemporary life. That is not correct. God's character does not change with our circumstances. Situations cannot alter God's standards of righteousness.

However, situations do influence the administration of God's commands. We must understand that the letter of the law is not to take precedence over the spirit and intent of the law.

God's administration of the Old Testament law concerning the making, consecration, and use of the showbread for worship illustrates this point. The bread was to be kept in the Tabernacle on the table before the Lord (Leviticus 24:5-9). But when David was fleeing from Saul, he and his men became hungry. When David asked the priest for bread, only the showbread was available. Yet the priest gave it to David (1 Samuel 21:1-6). This was a clear violation of the letter of the law.

Jesus interpreted this Old Testament incident when the Pharisees questioned him about the hungry disciples picking grain on the Sabbath. In the Pharisees' minds this was a violation of the command to do no work on the Sabbath. Christ said, "Have you not read what David did, when he became hungry, he and his companions . . . ate the consecrated bread, which was not lawful . . . but if you had known what this means, 'I desire compassion and not a sacrifice,' you would not have condemned the innocent" (Matthew 12:1-8 NASB). Christ's explanation was clear. The consecration of Tabernacle bread or working on the Lord's Day was never intended to interfere with caring for the hungry. God's principle was to meet genuine human need. The principle was absolute; but the application was adapted to the specific situation. We must similarly interpret the spirit of the law in daily business decisions.

At first glance this might seem like an easy way out. In reality it is not. Following the spirit of God's laws calls us to a higher standard than just following them legalistically. Jesus illustrated this when he compared the Old Testament law with his better way in the Sermon on the Mount.

You have heard that it was said, Eye for eye and tooth for tooth. But I tell you, Do not resist an evil person. If someone strikes you on the right cheek, turn to him the other also. And if someone wants to sue you and take your tunic, let him have your cloak as well. If someone forces you to go one mile, go with him two miles. Give to the one who asks you, and do not turn away from the one who wants to borrow from you. (Matthew 5:38–42)

Following the spirit of that passage in business is tough. It requires all the wisdom and courage we can muster.

Fallacies of Simplistic Thinking

God's commands do not do away with our need to make moral judgments. For example, God does not condone stealing. It is easy to apply this principle to know that stealing an automobile to take a joy ride is wrong. Other situations require more difficult judgments and analysis. Polaroid and Eastman Kodak battled in the courts for years because Kodak developed an instant film process similar to Polaroid's. Kodak said its process was different and thus a separate invention. Polaroid claimed that it was stolen. The courts currently agree with Polaroid and reject the argument of Eastman Kodak. Even so, the issue is not settled. This decision by a lower court is under appeal. Is Kodak's slightly different product a new product? How do we interpret God's commandment against stealing in this situation?

Moral choices do not always involve choices between one thing that is wrong and another that is right. Often choices are between two or more "rights." Let's examine business decisions relating to the use of profits. Should they be used to increase wages, cut prices, reinvest in capital equipment, or increase the owner's dividends? The morally superior alternative is not completely clear, since any of the choices will benefit some stakeholder group.

In our world, which is dominated by sin, we also confront choices in which none of the alternatives are good. When a business faces economic difficulty it is often necessary to decide between laying employees off or letting the business go further into decline. Many business decisions are tradeoffs between what is good for the company or what is good for an individual employee; or between safety and cost of manufacture; or between quality and price. Sometimes we must ask which is the lesser of two evils.

Once we have interpreted the Bible, developed the courage to do what is right, and analyzed the trade-offs, we still have to deal with our limited knowledge. Because of our ignorance we cannot always anticipate a bad chain of events that may result from our decision. For example, we might seem like poor stewards if we bought stock in a company that later lost money because of factors we didn't know when we bought the stock. Or we might, in our drive to be impeccably honest, choose to release information about warranty problems, ultimately causing sales to plummet and jobs to be lost. Even with the best of intentions we can make terrible mistakes.

We also experience tension because of our low level of confidence in God's support. We flinch and waffle when we perceive moral tension and risk ahead. We are tempted to doubt that God will help us when we obey his moral absolutes.

Abraham's absolute trust in God's promise that, ". . . through Isaac your offspring will be reckoned" (Genesis 21:12; Hebrews 11:18), enabled him to obey God. He stood the test of offering his only son as a sacrifice. Abraham was confident that God would be faithful to his covenant by raising Isaac from the dead (Hebrews 11:19), even though rational thought and experience could have convinced Abraham otherwise. This confidence lay behind his willingness to sacrifice Isaac (Genesis 22:1–19).

Ethical Means and Ends

Given these complexities, how can we practically improve our ethics in business? We should begin by remembering to evaluate whether or not the goals we want to achieve and the means we choose to achieve them are acceptable to God. Quite likely we agree that our purposes must be moral. We would not deliberately set out to cheat customers, to run competitors into the ground, to harm the community, to belittle employees, or to disregard stockholders. As Christians we easily understand that our objectives must reflect God's laws.

It is more difficult to sort through the various means that can be used to reach goals. Although we've heard the phrase "The ends do not justify the means," we don't always know how to apply that in a given situation. One helpful distinction may be to separate means into those which involve moral principles and those which involve preferences. Intentionally ignoring employee safety to keep down costs involves a moral principle. Requiring a person to do the tedious job of reshelving picked-over merchandise involves only preference. All of us need to do things we would rather not do. We can accept that in an imperfect world; but we should not violate a moral principle to accomplish even good ends.

It is important to find ways to get help in working through ambiguous issues. Sometimes we are so close to a situation that we lose sensitivity. We should discuss issues with managers and business peers outside our own firm. Members of our church and our pastor can be helpful. Such counsel may not solve our ethical dilemmas, but it will help us find the most ethical strategy or alternatives we may have overlooked.

It is very important to plan. When we sense that an ethically sensitive situation is ahead, we should sort out the strategies and possible consequences in advance. Many ethical disasters can be avoided if we shape formal ethics policies and educate our employees about ethical responses before the actual situation confronts them. It is difficult to be ethically sensitive in the heat of making a tough decision. Many companies have developed statements of ethical guidelines for employees to use when facing tough decisions. By working ahead we can often avoid the horns of the ethical dilemma. With careful analysis, discussions with others, planning, and God's help we can improve the ethics of our business practices.

Our Response in Obedience

God's absolutes—commands to love God, love our neighbors, do justice, love kindness, walk humbly with God—provide us with absolute principles that guide every situation. They reflect the righteousness of God. Only God has absolutely pure motives and can accomplish what is absolutely right. God also declares absolute standards. God's moral standards are not relative, even though the way we apply them does change to fit unique circumstances.

Doing business in a way that reflects the righteousness of God is not easy. It requires all the courage and wisdom we can develop. The key to developing that strength and wisdom is a strong, growing, vital relationship to Jesus Christ.

We will find strength by becoming more like Christ. God calls us to put off the old self and put on the new self (Ephesians 4:22–24). "Seeing" Christ transforms our innermost being, our heart, character, and thoughts (1 John 3:2; 2 Corinthians 3:18; Ephesians 1:18). This seeing is under the control of God. It is not a do-it-yourself project. At the same time, however, ". . . if [we] seek him, he will let [us] find him . . ." (2 Chronicles 15:2 NASB). We are told if we draw near to him, he will draw near to us (James 4:8).

To be like Christ we must know Christ—not as a philosophy or ideal concept, but as the living Lord of our lives. This includes obedience. In fact we cannot know Christ unless we do obey him. As we become more obedient, Christ will further reveal himself to us (John 15:9, 10).

Growing in Christ is an ongoing, interactive process. Christ reveals his love, and we respond in loving obedience. He teaches us more; we experience his grace and become more deeply committed to following him.

God has given us absolute moral principles. They may not seem real to people who are not committed to Jesus Christ, but they are very real to Christians who know Christ. The existence of absolute standards and principles does not eliminate the need for us to make difficult moral judgments. We must still use good judgment and analysis to determine what is actually just, what is really fair, and what is truly honest. We are free to make choices and decisions that will not always have perfectly good consequences. God is merciful and will forgive us if we make mistakes as we grow in faith and practice anchored in Jesus Christ.

QUESTIONS FOR REFLECTION

Business Bluffing

1. In what ways do you agree with Carr? In what ways do you disagree?
2. What are the dangers of looking at business as a game like poker?
3. Are there areas of your life in which you use Carr's approach?
4. Many people will argue that "honesty is the best policy." Do you agree? If you do, is that enough reason to try to be honest? Are there other reasons?

Exploring the Bible

1. What does Matthew 6:33 suggest about truth telling? Is it possible to tell the simple truth in advertising, employee evaluations, conversations with competitors, and annual financial reports?
2. Use a concordance to find the many times love of neighbor is discussed in the Bible. The command to love is clear. Think of biblical stories where love is expressed. Note the exciting ways love is expressed.

Contemporary Comment

1. There are many questions to which there are no specific biblical answers. How do Christians discover what is right in these situations?

2. Discuss how each of the following resources is helpful in responding in moral ways to important practical questions.

- the Bible
- the Holy Spirit
- the example of Jesus
- church congregation
- past experience
- academic analysis

3. How can Christians adjust their actions to situational factors yet avoid the dangers of relativism?

NOTES

1. Albert Z. Carr, "Is Business Bluffing Ethical?" *Harvard Business Review* (January/February, 1968): 143–153. Used with permission.

FOR FURTHER READING

Chapter 1

Louis Berkhof, "Common Grace," in *Manual of Reformed Doctrine* (Grand Rapids, MI: William B. Eerdmans, 1933), 224–29.

Brian Griffiths, "Is Christianity Relevant?" in Brian Griffiths's *Morality and the Marketplace, London Lectures in Contemporary Christianity* (London: Hodder and Stoughton, 1980), chapter 3.

Arthur Holmes, ed., *The Making of a Christian Mind: A Christian World View and the Academic Enterprise* (Downers Grove, IL: InterVarsity Press, 1985).

Thomas J. Peters and Robert H. Waterman, *In Search of Excellence* (New York: Harper & Row, 1982).

Chapter 2

Carl Kreider, "A Christian Standard of Living," in *The Christian Entrepreneur* (Scottdale, PA: Herald Press, 1980), chapter 5.

Francis A. Schaeffer, *No Little People* (Downers Grove, IL: InterVarsity Press, 1977).

Thorstein Veblen, *Theory of the Leisure Class* (New York: Penguin, 1979).

Marion Wade, "Christian Vitality and Teamwork Make Business a Ministry," in *The Lord is My Counsel* (New York: Prentice Hall, 1966), chapter 5.

Chapter 3

United States Catholic Conference, *Economic Justice for All: Catholic Social Teaching and the U.S. Economy*, 3d draft (Washington, DC: United States Catholic Conference, 1986).

Donald B. Kraybill, *The Upside-Down Kingdom* (Scottdale, PA: Herald Press, 1973).

R. C. Sproul, *Stronger Than Steel: The Wayne Alderson Story* (San Francisco: Harper & Row, 1980).

Chapter 4

H. M. Kuitert, "The Image of God," in *Signals from the Bible* (Grand Rapids, MI: William B. Eerdmans, 1972), 30–33.

John Laidlaw, *The Biblical Doctrine of Man* (Edinburgh: T & T Clark, 1895).

Robert Merton, *Social Theory and Social Structure* (New York: Free Press, 1968).

David G. Myers and Malcolm A. Jeeves, "Nice People and Evil Doers" in *Psychology Through the Eyes of Faith* (San Francisco: Harper & Row, 1987), chapter 26.

Chapter 5

Hugh DePree, "People as Bearers of Responsibility," in *Business as Unusual, the People and Principles at Herman Miller* (Zeeland, MI: Herman Miller, Inc., 1986), 117–135.

William T. Kirwan, *Biblical Concepts for Christian Counselling: A Case for Integrating Psychology and Theology* (Grand Rapids, MI: Baker Book House, 1984).

Abraham Maslow, *Motivation and Personality* (New York: Harper & Row, 1970).

David G. Myers and Malcolm A. Jeeves, "Personality," in *Psychology Through the Eyes of Faith* (San Francisco: Harper & Row, 1987), Chapter 12.

Lawrence Peter and Raymond Hull, *The Peter Principle* (New York: Bantam, 1984).

Chapter 6

Sir Frederick Catherwood, "The Christian as an Employer," in *The Christian in Industrial Society* (Leicester, England: InterVarsity Press, 1964), chapter 10.

Carl Kreider, "Christian Ethics in Business: Specific Applications," in *The Christian Entrepreneur* (Scottdale, PA: Herald Press, 1980), chapter 4.

Douglas McGregor, *The Human Side of Enterprise*, New York: McGraw Hill, 1960.

Francis Schaeffer, *No Little People: Sixteen Sermons for the Twentieth Century* (Downers Grove, IL: InterVarsity Press, 1974).

Robert E. Speer and John J. Eagan, *A Memoir of an Adventure for the Kingdom of God on Earth* (Birmingham, AL: American Cast Iron Pipe Company, P.O. Box 2727, Birmingham, AL 35202, 1939; reprinted 1976). Available privately from the American Cast Iron Pipe Company, P.O. Box 2727, Birmingham, AL 35202.

Chapter 7

Carl F. H. Henry, *Aspects of Christian Social Ethics* (Grand Rapids, MI: Baker Book House, 1980), chapter 2.

John R. W. Stott, "Creative by Creation: Our Need for Work," *Christianity Today* (June 8, 1979): 32–33.

Patricia Ward and Marti Stout, "Vocation," in *Christian Women at Work* (Grand Rapids, MI: Zondervan, 1981), chapter 3.

Chapter 8

John Bernbaum and Simon Steer, *Why Work? Careers and Employment in Biblical Perspective* (Grand Rapids, MI: Baker Book House, 1986), chapters 1 and 2.

Paul Goodman, *Growing Up Absurd* (New York: Random House, 1962).

Lee Hardy, *The Fabric of This World* (Grand Rapids, MI: William B. Eerdmans, 1990).

Donald R. Heiges, *The Christian Calling* (Philadelphia, PA: Fortress Press, 1984).

William G. Ouchi, *Theory Z* (New York: Avon Books, 1982).

Chapter 9

Max DePree, "Theory Fastball," in *Leadership Is An Art* (New York: Doubleday and Co., Inc., 1989), 31–42.

John Warwick Montgomery, *Human Rights and Human Dignity* (Grand Rapids, MI: Zondervan, 1986).

Nicholas Wolterstorff, *Until Justice and Peace Embrace* (Grand Rapids, MI: William B. Eerdmans, 1983), 82–85.

Chapter 10

John W. Alexander, *Managing Our Work* (Downers Grove, IL: InterVarsity Press, 1978).

Kenneth Gangel, "Bureaucracy and the Christian Organization," in *Competent to Lead* (Chicago, IL: Moody Bible Institute, 1974), chapter 5.

Myron Rush, "The Team Spirit," and "Decision Making Problem Solving," in *Management: A Biblical Approach* (Wheaton, IL: Victor Books, 1978), chapters 4 and 7.

Chapter 11

Warren Bennis and Burt Nanus, *Leaders* (New York: Harper & Row, 1985).

Max De Pree, *Leadership Is An Art* (New York: Doubleday and Co., Inc., 1989).

Robert Greenleaf, *Servant Leadership* (New York: Paulist Press, 1977).

J. Oswald Sanders, *Paul the Leader* (Colorado Springs, CO: NAVPRESS, 1984).

Chapter 12

Kenneth O. Gangel, "The Use and Abuse of Power," in *Competent to Lead* (Chicago, IL: Moody Bible Institute, 1974), chapter 9.

Clinton W. McLemore, *Good Guys Finish First* (Philadelphia, PA: Westminster Press, 1983).

Patricia Ward and Martha Stout, "Working Within Organizations," in *Christian Women at Work* (Grand Rapids, MI: Zondervan, 1981), chapter 8.

Chapter 13

Robert Bellah, *Habits of the Heart* (New York: Harper & Row, 1986).

William Diehl, "Life in Community," in *In Search of Faithfulness, Lessons from the Christian Community* (Philadelphia, PA: Fortress Press, 1987), chapter 7.

Ted W. Engstrom and Edward R. Dayton, "Let's Be Accountable," in *The Art of Management for Christian Leaders* (Waco, TX: Word Books, 1976), chapter 8.

John C. Purdy, *Parables at Work* (Philadelphia, PA: Westminster Press, 1985).

Chapter 14

Frederick Herzberg, Bernard Mauser, and Barbara B. Snyderman, *The Motivation to Work* (New York: Wiley, 1959).

Chua Wee Hian, *Making of a Leader* (Downers Grove, IL: InterVarsity Press, 1987).

Kenneth Lipper, *Wall Street*, New York: Berkley Publishers, 1988.

David G. Myers and Malcolm A. Jeeves, "Behavior and Attitudes —Action and Faith," in *Psychology Through the Eyes of Faith* (San Francisco: Harper & Row, 1987), chapter 27.

Judith Allen Shelly, "God's Call to Work," in *Not Just a Job* (Downers Grove, IL: InterVarsity Press, 1985), chapter 1.

Chapter 15

Ted W. Engstrom and Edward R. Dayton, "Communicate, or Else . . . ," in *The Art of Management for Christian Leaders* (Waco, TX: Word Books, 1976), chapter 13.

J. Grant Howard, *The Trauma of Transparency: A Biblical Approach to Inter-Personal Communication* (Portland, OR: Multnomah Press, 1979).

Myron Rush, "Successful Communication Skills," in *Management: A Biblical Approach* (Wheaton, IL: Victor Books, 1978), chapter 8.

Robert H. Waterman, *The Renewal Factor* (New York: Bantam Books, Inc., 1987).

Chapter 16

Tom L. Beauchamp, and Norman E. Bowie, eds., "Corporate Social Responsibility," in *Ethical Theory and Business*, 2d ed. (Englewood Cliffs, NJ: Prentice-Hall, 1983), section 2, 52–127.

Charles K. Wilber and Kenneth P. Jameson, "Toward A New Social Contract," in *An Inquiry into the Poverty of Economics* (Notre Dame, IN: University of Notre Dame Press, 1983), chapter 28.

Nicholas Wolterstorff, "For Justice in Shalom" in *Until Justice and Peace Embrace* (Grand Rapids, MI: William B. Eerdmans, 1983), 69–72.

Chapter 17

Carl Kreider, "How Much Shall I Give to the Church?" in *The Christian Entrepreneur* (Scottdale, PA: Herald Press, 1980), chapter 6.

Michael Porter, *Competitive Strategy: Techniques for Analyzing Industries and Competitors* (New York: Free Press, 1980).

Marion Wade, "The Competition is You" and "Love Casts Out Fear—Even of Competition," in *The Lord is My Counsel* (New York: Prentice Hall, 1966), chapters 7 and 10.

Oliver F. Williams and John W. Houck, *Full Value: Cases in Christian Business Ethics* (San Francisco: Harper & Row, 1978).

Chapter 18

E. Calvin Beisner, *Prosperity and Poverty: A Compassionate Use of Resources in a World of Scarcity* (Westchester, IL: Crossway Books, 1988), chapters 4 and 5.

Brian Griffiths, *The Creation of Wealth* (Downers Grove, IL: InterVarsity Press, 1984).

Carl Kreider, *The Rich and the Poor—A Christian Perspective on Global Economics* (Scottdale, PA: Herald Press, 1987).

Chapter 19

Stephen Charnock, "On the Immutability of God," *Discourses Upon the Existence and Attributes of God*, volume 1 (Grand Rapids, MI: Baker Book House, 1981), Discourse IV.

Richard Chewning, *Business Ethics in a Changing Culture* (Reston, VA: Reston Publishing, 1984).

John W. Williams and Oliver F. Houck, *Full Value, Cases in Christian Business Ethics* (San Francisco: Harper & Row, 1978).

A BIBLIOGRAPHY OF ADDITIONAL RESOURCES

The Christian business community and Christian business faculty are developing resources and support groups to expand Christian perspectives in business. The following are selected lists of materials and groups with distinctly Christian concerns about business. A more complete and continuously expanding resource list is available through the Christian Business Faculty Association, whose address is included below.

Books

Catherwood, H. F. R. *The Christian from 9 to 5*. Grand Rapids, MI: Zondervan, 1983.

Diehl, William. *Thank God It's Monday*. Philadelphia, PA: Fortress Press, 1982.

Garrett, Thomas M., and Richard J. Klonoski. *Business Ethics*. New York: Prentice Hall, 1986.

Graham, W. Fred, George N. Monsma, Jr., Carl J. Sinke, Alan Storkey, John P. Tiemstra. *Reforming Economics; A Christian Perspective on Economic Theory and Practice*. Lewiston, NY: Edwin Mellen Press, publication forthcoming.

Hay, Donald. *Economics Today: A Christian Critique*. Grand Rapids, MI: William B. Eerdmans, publication forthcoming.

Hind, James R. *The Heart and Soul of Effective Management: A Christian Approach to Managing and Motivating People*. Wheaton, IL: Victor Books, 1989.

Houck, John W., and Oliver F. Williams, eds. *Co-creation and Capitalism: John Paul II's Laborem exercens*. Lanham, MD: University Press of America, 1983.

Klay, Robin Kendrick. *Counting the Cost: The Economics of Christian Stewardship*. Grand Rapids, MI: William B. Eerdmans, 1987.

Lincoln, James F. *A New Approach to Industrial Economics*. Greenwich, CT: Devin Adair Publishing, 1961.

Novak, Michael. *The Spirit of Democratic Capitalism*. New York: Simon and Schuster, 1982.

Rossi, Sanna Barlow. *Anthony T. Rossi, Christian and Entrepreneur*. Downers Grove, IL: InterVarsity Press, 1986.

Rush, Myron. *Lord of the Marketplace*. Wheaton, IL: Victor Books, 1986.

Ryken, Leland. *Christian Perspectives on Work and Leisure*. Portland, OR: Multnomah Press, 1987.

Stackhouse, Max. *Public Theology and Political Economy*. Grand Rapids, MI: William B. Eerdmans, 1987.

Walton, William B. *Innkeeper, A Co-founder of Holiday Inns, Inc*. Wheaton, IL: Tyndale Houses, 1987.

Williams, Oliver F., and John W. Houck. *The Judeo-Christian Vision and the Modern Corporation*. Notre Dame, IN: University of Notre Dame, 1982.

Mass Media

Accountability to the Church. 1989. Distributed by Precision Audio, Inc., 18582 U.S. Route 20, Bristol, IN 46507. Audiocassette, 30 min. Dennis Bakke discusses the relationship of businesspersons to the church.

Biblical Justice. 1984. Distributed by the Christian College Coalition, Washington, D.C. Videocassette, 45 min. A discussion of justice in relationship to business and economic issues.

Bruised Camels. 1987. Distributed by InterVarsity Christian Fellowship, Madison, WI. Audiocassette, 60 min. A narrative about building support groups for Christians in business.

Called to the Marketplace. 1987. Distributed by InterVarsity Christian Fellowship, Madison, WI. Four videocassettes, each 20–30 min. An examination of Christian roles in paid occupations within secular society.

God and Profit? Building a Large Corporation on Biblical Values. 1984. Distributed by the Christian College Coalition, Washington, D.C. Videocassette, 30 min. A discussion of Christian corporate goals and their implementation in Service Master, Inc.

Management: A Biblical Approach. 1987. Distributed by Scripture Press, Wheaton, IL. Two audiocassettes, each 60 min. Practical advice on the implementation of a biblical philosophy of management.

The Miracle of Pittron. 1980. Distributed by Value of the Person Consultants, Pittsburgh, PA. Film, 16 mm, 58 min. The story of Wayne Alderson's Christian efforts to overcome labor/management tensions in Pittron Steel Corporation.

Newsletters

Advocate. Addresses issues of law and public policy from a Christian perspective. Includes some business and economic articles and references. Available from Evangelicals for Social Action, Lancaster and City Avenues, Philadelphia, PA 19151.

Bread for the World. Addresses Christian concerns about poverty and hunger, both nationally and internationally. Available from Bread for the World, 802 Rhode Island Avenue, NE, Washington, D.C. 20018.

Centering. Focuses on bringing lay professionals into the ministry of the church. Available from Center for Ministry of the Laity, Andover Newton Theological School, 210 Herrick Rd., Newton Centre, MA 02159.

Fellowship Report. Addresses Christian chief executive officers on biblical principles. Available from Fellowship of Companies for Christ International, 2920 Brandywine Rd., Colgate Bldg., Suite 150, Atlanta, GA 30341.

The Marketplace. Addresses Christian approaches to business and to economic development. Available from Mennonite Economic Development Associates, P.O. Box M, Akron, PA 17501.

Network Fellowship Newsletter. Addresses the concerns of Christians in business. Available from Fred Smith Associates, 1111 N. Mockingbird Lane, Suite 1342, Dallas, TX 78029.

Networks. Addresses Christian approaches to work in a secular environment. Available from Marketplace, InterVarsity Christian Fellowship, P.O. Box 7895, Madison, WI 53707-7895.

Perspective. A devotional newsletter available from Dr. Richard Halverson, U.S. Senate Chaplain, P.O. Box 7800, McLean, VA 22106-7800.

Public Justice Report. Explores both foreign and domestic public policy and contains relevant articles on poverty and on the environment. Available from Center for Public Justice, 806 Fifteenth St. NW, Suite 440, Washington, D.C. 20005.

Spiritual Fitness in Business. Considers the development of a Christian lifestyle within the business context. Available from Spiritual

Fitness in Business, 1900 Firman Dr., Suite 100, Richardson, TX 75081.

Support and Development Groups

Center for Ethics and Corporate Policy. 637 South Dearborn Street, Chicago, IL 60605. Phone (312) 922-1512.

Center for Ministry of the Laity. Andover Newton Theological School, 210 Herrick Rd., Newton Centre, MA 02159. Phone (617) 964-1100.

Christian Business Faculty Association. For membership and newsletter contact Fred Luurtsema, Geneva College, Beaver Falls, PA 15010. Phone (412) 847-6619.

Christian Business Men's Committee (CBMC). 1800 McCallie, P.O. Box 3308, Chattanooga, TN 37404.

Christian Labour Association of Canada. Work Research Foundation. Christian Labour Association of Canada, 8212 Albion Road, Rexdale, Toronto, Ontario, Canada, M9V 1A3.

Fellowship of Companies for Christ International. 2920 Brandywine Rd., Colgate Bldg., Suite 150, Atlanta, GA 30341.

Institute for Christian Organization Development. Contact Dr. Pat LaTore, Fuller Theological Seminary, 135 N. Oakland, Pasadena, CA 91182. Phone (818) 584-5200.

Intercristo, A Division of Christa Ministries. 19303 Fremont Avenue North, Seattle, WA 98133-3800. Phone 1(800) 426-1343.

KingBay Chaplaincy. P.O. Box 175, Room 204, Commercial Union Tower, Dominion Center, Toronto, Canada, M5K 1H6. Phone (416) 366-0818.

Labor/Management Prayer Breakfast. Held annually in Pittsburgh, PA. Contact Value of the Person Consultants, 100 Ross St., Pittsburgh, PA 15219. Phone (412) 562-9070.

Laity Lodge. P.O. Box 670, Kerrville, TX 78029.

Marketplace Ministries. InterVarsity Christian Fellowship, P.O. Box 7895, Madison, WI 53707-7895.

Professional Women's Fellowship. 219 First Ave. N., #342, Seattle, WA 98109. Phone (206) 382-7276.

Reformed Christian Business and Professional Association. 970 Bonnieview Ave., Burlington, Ontario, Canada, L7T 1T5. Phone (416) 524-1203.

The Servant Society. 900 Calle de los Amigos, #D-502, Santa Barbara, CA 93105. Phone (805) 687-2199.

Trinity Center for Ethics and Corporate Policy. 74 Trinity Place, New York, NY 10006. Phone (212) 602-0816.

Workplace Ministry. St. Andrews-Wesley Church, 1012 Nelson Street, Vancouver, B.C., Canada, V6E 1H8. Phone (604) 683-4574.

INDEX